Butterfly Economics

A New General Theory of Social and Economic Behaviour

PAUL ORMEROD

faber and faber

First published in 1998
by Faber and Faber Limited
3 Queen Square WC1N 3AU

Photoset by Parker Typesetting Service, Leicester
Printed in England by Clays Ltd, St Ives Plc, Bungay, Suffolk

© Paul Ormerod, 1998

Paul Ormerod is hereby identified as author
of this work in accordance with Section 77
of the Copyright, Designs and Patents Act 1988

A CIP record for this book
is available from the British Library

ISBN 0–571–19005–7 (cased)
0–571–20041–9 (export paperback)

2 4 6 8 10 9 7 5 3 1

BUTTERFLY ECONOMICS

Contents

Preface

My previous book, *The Death of Economics*, was first published in 1994. My aim was to provide a critique of conventional economics which was accessible to general readers. Economics occupies a dominant position in public policy around the world and, having trained as a professional economist, I felt that its secrets should be more widely shared. Judging by the response to the book around the world, I would like to think that this aim was met. A secondary objective was to suggest how economics could be developed to give a better understanding of how the world actually operates. The study of human societies and economies is of great importance, and it is incumbent upon critics of orthodoxy to advance alternative ways of making progress.

Butterfly Economics contains the development of my thinking over the past few years. Again, it is addressed primarily to members of the general public. Economic and social issues affect everyone, and it is important for all informed citizens to reflect upon them.

An argument which I made nearly a decade ago is that conventional economics is mistaken when it views the economy and society as a machine, whose behaviour, no matter how complicated, is ultimately predictable and controllable. On the contrary, human society is much more like a living organism – a living creature, whose behaviour can only be understood by looking at the complex interactions of its individual parts. It is this concept and its implications which form the underlying theme of *Butterfly Economics*.

My fellow economists – although I prefer the term 'political economists' which Adam Smith and the founding fathers used to describe themselves – may take more comfort in this book than in my previous one. A motif running throughout, and primarily addressed to them, is that conventional economics is a special case of the more general class of models which it is now feasible to build. In orthodox economics, individuals are not permitted to affect each other's behaviour directly, and in circumstances where this is a good approximation to reality, this offers a powerful explanation of what goes on. But such circumstances are rather limited, and it is more usually the case that people or companies are influenced directly by what others do. This leads to a much more complex world, but one which offers a better description of reality. Economics and the other social sciences will, I believe, eventually adopt this model.

Throughout *Butterfly Economics*, a contrast is made between conventional, machine-like ways of analysing problems, and the more biologically oriented concepts which I advance. It is important to make such comparisons, but the process of so doing can occasionally demand some effort on the part of the reader. This is particularly so with chapters 8 and 9, which discuss the crucial concept of the business cycle. These are probably the hardest chapters for the general reader, but are in a number of ways the most important of the book. For they show how viewing the economy as a living creature enables progress to be made in understanding the business cycle, an integral feature of all market economies and one which conventional economics finds particularly hard to explain satisfactorily.

I am grateful to a number of people for encouragement and discussions which have helped to develop the ideas of this book, and in particular to Michael Campbell, Robin Marris, Bridget Rosewell and Bob Rowthorn. I have also been stimulated for a number of years by the work of Richard Goodwin, who sadly died in 1997. Julian Loose and his colleagues at Faber and Faber have once again provided valuable editorial support.

Paul Ormerod
London and Wiltshire, July 1998

Introduction

The conventional ways of thinking in the social sciences, and in economics in particular, offer at best a partial and at worst a misleading view of how the world operates. In essence, the world is seen as a machine. The machine may be very complicated, but in principle it can be understood completely, and the consequences of using it in various ways can be predicted. A lever pulled here or a button pressed there will have entirely predictable consequences.

The failure of such conventional thinking to explain events can be seen each Christmas. Whether it is Buzz Lightyear or Ninja Turtles, Teletubbies or Cabbage Patch dolls, the level of demand for the toy which becomes the *ne plus ultra* of every child's Christmas stocking almost invariably runs far ahead of the supply. Shops are stripped of all their stocks, and the toy becomes simply unavailable. Firms appear to be congenitally incapable of anticipating the level of sales.

In just the same way, enormous uncertainty and difficulty of prediction appear to be inherent in the film industry. Even the existence of major Hollywood stars and a huge advertising budget is no guarantee of success. In contrast, improbable low-budget movies such as *The Full Monty* and *Anaconda* – the latter being dismissed memorably by a critic as a 'movie about huge snakes devouring a B-grade cast' – occasionally become major successes.

Consumer markets such as those for Christmas toys or films raise serious problems for conventional economic theory. In such theory the tastes and preferences of individuals are fixed, and prices are supposed to adjust in a mechanical way to balance out supply and demand. But in the film or Christmas toy industries, when a new release or product is issued, consumers do not know in advance whether they will like it or loathe it. People have to learn what their own preferences are, and the choice of any individual is influenced powerfully by the opinions and actions of others. Popular toys or films become even more popular precisely because they are popular. Hence the enormous differences seen in revenues between the most and least successful films, and the spectacular bursts in demand for a single product which occur almost every year at Christmas.

Conventional approaches to the analysis of the economy and of society must be altered fundamentally if we are to make progress in understanding both how world operates, and how we might try to change it for the better. Economies and societies are not machines. They are more like living organisms. Individuals do not act in isolation, but affect each other in complex ways.

The title of this book – *Butterfly Economics* – emphasizes this fundamental view of society as a living creature, which adapts and learns. The behaviour of the system as a whole can never be understood by mechanistically adding together its component parts: just as a living creature is more than the sum of the individual cells which make up its body, so the economy and society are more than the sum of the individuals who inhabit it. The image of the butterfly also draws upon popular ideas of chaos theory, in which the beating of the wings of a butterfly can in principle cause a tornado on the other side of the globe. The key theme of my book is to take these ideas even further in the practical context of modern economies and societies. These are complex systems which hover on the brink of chaos.

The butterfly emphasizes the non-mechanistic nature of my thinking, yet, paradoxically, the ideas I advance in the book demand the use of far more modern mathematics than is the case in conventional economics, which remains fixated with the maths of nineteenth-century engineers. Readers are immediately reassured that the main text of the book consists entirely of words and not equations. But the complex inter-relations between the behaviour of individuals and the overall outcome lead to arguments of subtlety and refinement which are underpinned by the new maths of the analysis of society.

In the living, constantly changing economic and social worlds, the connection between the size of an event and the magnitude of its effects is no longer routine and mechanical. Small changes often have small consequences, but occasionally these are large, and from time to time dramatic. Equally, large changes sometimes have large effects, but they may also make surprisingly little difference to the eventual outcome. An important implication of the often blurred, unfocused connection between events and their effects is that predicting what will happen in the immediate future with any degree of accuracy is at best very difficult and sometimes impossible.

Yet in the longer run, there *is* considerable regularity of behaviour. The often unpredictable interactions between individuals lead to a certain kind of self-regulation in the behaviour of the system as a whole. We cannot say exactly where the system will be at any point in time, but we can often set bounds around the areas in which it will move.

The analysis of the economy and society which I advance in this book illuminates a world of paradox and subtlety. The key to a better understanding of many economic and social phenomena lies in a seemingly innocuous observation, already introduced by the examples of Christmas toys and Hollywood. Namely, that the behaviour of an individual can be directly affected by the behaviour of others. In other words, people see what others do, and may be influenced by it.

Trivial and obvious though this idea may seem, it leads to situations of great analytical complexity. In contrast, orthodox economics is forced to assume that the tastes and preferences of individuals are completely fixed. For all its apparent sophistication, its machine-oriented maths cannot cope with situations in which these can change according to how others behave. Systems in which individuals copy each other's behaviour require different techniques of analysis – mathematical techniques only available during the past ten to fifteen years, and the new power of computers to simulate artificially the behaviour of such societies.

The apparently straightforward assumption that individuals live in society and can be influenced directly by the behaviour of others has profound implications for the conduct of public policy. Once we think of the economy and society as a complex, living system, the frequent failures of policy can be readily understood. These systems are inherently extremely difficult to predict and control. This is not merely a point of intellectual interest, but of great practical import. For it implies that much of the control which governments believe they exercise over the economy and society is illusory.

The fundamental difficulties of short-term prediction in complex systems mean that it is not a matter of thinking of cleverer, more sophisticated ways of carrying out forecasts. In the current state of scientific knowledge, it is simply not possible to carry out forecasts which are systematically accurate over a period of time. An individual prediction may prove to be broadly correct, but in a series of such predictions, substantial errors will inevitably be made. In a world in which the difficulties of short-term prediction are deep and intrinsic, any efforts by governments to intervene and alter the immediate outcome are unlikely to meet with very much success.

The problems of predictability which arise across all the social sciences are often attributed to the non-controllable nature of experiments in the social, compared to the natural, sciences. This is certainly a formidable practical difficulty. But my argument goes beyond this. Unpredictability is an inherent part of the processes which underlie a very wide range of economic and social phenomena.

Governments of all political persuasions have come to play an ever-increasing role in our lives, as they grapple with multifarious problems whose persistence make the labours of Hercules look like child's play in comparison. In Britain and America there has been some check to the growth of the public sector in recent years, but the sheer size of government is by historical standards enormous.

The New Deal was bitterly vilified as socialism in the 1930s, but spending by the US Federal government at that time was less than 6 per cent of the overall economy. The state's share of the economy in Britain under Margaret Thatcher was considerably higher than it was under the most openly socialist administration in the country's history, that of Clement Attlee in the late 1940s. But it is not just in terms of spending that government has become bigger – restrictions, regulations and legislative controls of various kinds have 'grow'd and grow'd' like Topsy.

Despite this huge growth in government activity, problems stubbornly remain. And the Law of Unintended Consequences often applies to policy actions: their impact either turns out to be the opposite of what is intended, or even if they succeed in their aims, there are unforeseen adverse consequences elsewhere.

This does not mean that governments are powerless, or that the economy and society have no structure at all. Far from it. There *is* regularity and self-organization, but not in the conventional ways. Governments should step back and take a wider perspective rather than constantly intervening. In terms of successful policies, less can be more.

Policy-makers have long been encouraged to believe in the check-list mentality which lies at the heart of conventional economics. Do A, B and C, and the consequence *will* be X. But this offers merely the illusion of control rather than the reality.

We need to change our perceptions of the role and power of governments. Much government intervention is motivated by specific, short-term ends, and depends crucially on the idea that the economy and/or society is a predictable machine. But accurate short-term prediction is at best difficult and at worst impossible. Small changes can have big consequences and vice versa. Policies can also have seemingly perverse effects. With a proper appreciation of how economies and societies work, the role of government is reduced whilst, paradoxically, its powers are increased.

We need to build on principles of thought drawn from biology rather than mechanics to get a better understanding of how the economy and society really work. The image of the butterfly is intended to reflect the softer, less dogmatic approach which is required. Other biological analogies are introduced in Chapter 1, which uses the example of the behaviour of an ant colony to describe many of the most important features which we need to understand. In Chapter 2, the ideas and concepts are applied directly to illuminate a range of apparently disparate problems – from why products with inferior technologies can often drive their superior rivals out of business to why financial markets are so dramatically volatile.

In Chapter 3, I switch focus away from economics to social questions, and use the theory of interacting agents to examine the problems of crime. Sudden changes can occur which are difficult to relate to changes in overall economic and social conditions. And in the case of crime there is the paradox that poverty is advanced as a reason for the soaring crime of the 1980s, yet the genuinely poverty-stricken 1930s were a period of very low crime rates. Chapter 4 looks at another key social question from the same perspective, namely the dramatic changes over the past thirty years in family structures in the West.

Chapter 5 steps back to look at the current state of economic theory, and offers examples of areas in which it can still be very helpful. But even on its own basis, the most elegant and advanced expressions of free market theory serve only to highlight its inadequacies.

Economic forecasting and attempts to control the economy by changes in taxation, public spending or interest rates remain a key part of government activity in the developed world. But the control which governments believe they have, in their ability both to make reasonably accurate forecasts and to understand the consequences of policy changes designed to alter the outcome, is largely illusory. Chapter 6 shows why this is so, and why the evidence is far more consistent with our complex world of interacting agents than it is with the mechanical world of conventional theory. Chapter 7 looks in a bit more detail at what some economists, particularly those who pop up in the media, claim they know about how government policy affects the economy. It argues that they do not actually know this at all, and gives some positive examples of what governments really can do.

There are two striking features of the Western market economies. First, there is slow but steady growth over very long periods of time. Second, there are persistent fluctuations – the booms and recessions of the business cycle – around this long-term trend. The phenomena of growth and the business cycle have occupied many of the best economists for over two hundred years, since the time of Adam Smith, and are absolutely central to our grasp of how the economy behaves. Their importance – both in practice and in theory – is reflected in the fact that a substantial part of the second half of the book, Chapters 8 to 12, is devoted to them. These chapters elucidate and explore the inadequacies of the orthodox approaches to business cycles and growth. But they also offer new theories based upon interacting agents, upon the basic principles of the world seen as a complex, living system, as alternative accounts of these fundamental features of capitalist economies.

Once we accept the idea that the behaviour of individuals can be affected directly by the actions of others, we move into an entirely different world from the conventional one of the social sciences. A wide range of seemingly disparate social and economic phenomena can be explained far more satisfactorily in this way than they can be by conventional thinking. Each one has its own nuances, but they are linked by their general implications. What is needed is a new, organic economics, one with a light touch, one sophisticated enough to allow for interaction – what, for the purposes of this book, I call 'Butterfly Economics'.

CHAPTER I

Living at the Edge of Chaos

Scientific research can often seem obscure and even pointless to out-
siders. This is not so much due to the intellectual difficulty involved in
understanding such activity, for it is widely accepted that this will
inevitably be the case. It is rather that many of the topics which are
examined seem to be almost designed to incur the scorn and wrath of the
lay person. Before sitting down this morning to write these very words,
for example, my eye fell on a report in a serious British newspaper. An
American psychologist had been visiting the country to carry out a study
of rams in the English Lake District. His research was complete. 'Ten per
cent of all rams', he proclaimed solemnly, 'are homosexual.' Readers no
doubt took consolation from the fact that this finding was obtained at the
expense of the American taxpayer and not themselves.

Nor are such examples confined exclusively to the sciences. I have long
admired Emily Brontë's novel *Wuthering Heights*. The opening chapters,
in which Lockwood first encounters the ill-tempered Heathcliff and his
assorted household, seem to me to be one of the finest pieces of comedy in
the whole corpus of English literature. Realizing that not everyone shares
this opinion, and in order to improve my understanding, I recently opened
a modern work of literary criticism on Brontë's masterpiece. It was
completely impenetrable. Many of the individual words were quite new to
me, and whole sentences, indeed whole pages, appeared to lack any
coherent meaning. I sought solace in the preface, where I learned that the
density of the text was deliberate. 'The analysis of literature and culture',
declared the author, 'is a task no less difficult, and no less demanding of a
specialized language, than the study of sub-atomic particles.' I hastened
immediately to a textbook on orthodox economic theory in an effort to
restore my sanity.

In the mid-1980s, entomologists carried out a series of experiments
with ants which, at first sight, appear equally esoteric. Two identical food

sources were placed at an equal distance from a nest of ants, and were constantly replenished so that they always remained identical. In other words, every time an ant removed a grain from one of the sources, another was added to the pile. And the two piles were exactly the same distance from the nest. How would the ant colony divide itself between the two sources of food?

The experiments appear at first sight to be of little or no interest to anyone outside the world of biology. Even among biologists, ant behaviour is a pretty specialized topic. Yet the results of the experiments turned out to be fiendishly difficult to explain, and a proper under-standing of them has widespread implications for behaviour far beyond that of the humble colony of ants, illuminating complex problems in human societies and economies, worlds living at the edge of chaos.

In the experiments there was, by design, absolutely no reason for the ants to prefer one of the sources to the other, so we might start by expecting that the ants would split evenly between them. A little reflection would lead us to think that, while this might very well be an outcome, any division would be possible. Suppose each ant emerges from the nest and visits one of the food piles at random. It is successful in obtaining food to bring back to the nest, and so on its next outing it has an incentive to revisit the site of its previous success. The pile is always replenished, so it will always obtain food from this site.

If this theory were correct, the distribution of the ants between the two piles could be analysed in just the same way as an experiment in tossing a fair coin and observing the split between heads and tails. The first time an ant comes out of the nest to look for food, its destination is given by the equivalent of a toss of a coin, and the design of the experiment gives it a strong incentive to keep revisiting its original choice. So, in theory, we could expect the colony to split in any proportion between the two piles. There would be a strong expectation that the split would be close to 50:50, because this is how a large number of tosses of a fair coin usually divide, but any distribution would be possible theoretically.

But the biologists had developed a more sophisticated version of this theory, based upon a known fact about ant behaviour. Once an ant has successfully found food – which it would, thanks to the design of the experiment – it will usually revisit the same site the next time and so on into the future. But when an ant which has found food returns to the nest, it physically stimulates another ant to follow it to the food source by chemical secretion. Some kinds of ant go even further and recruit whole groups to follow them, by laying a trail of secretions. So an ant emerging from the nest for the first time would be influenced in its decision by the trails of the ants it encounters on its journey.

In economic terms this means the behaviour of agents is influenced directly by the behaviour of others. In this example, the interaction between ants takes place at what we term the *local* level. No ant can ever observe the overall division of the colony between the two food sources, and so this cannot influence the choice of destination. But each ant is open to recruitment by the limited number of other ants which pass its immediate neighbourhood.

The situation is one in which, to introduce a technical term, positive feedback predominates. An ant goes out, finds food and encourages others to follow it back to its source. In this artificial experiment, the self-reinforcing mechanism is very strong, for each pile of food is constantly replenished. So the ants which are recruited find food with complete certainty, and return to recruit others. The more ants that visit any particular site, the greater the chance that yet more of them will visit it in future.

In other words, the consequences of actions by individual ants are enhanced by their influence on the behaviour of others, hence the phrase 'positive feedback'. The term is purely descriptive, and does not carry any overtones of approval or desirability. It applies to any system, such as that of our ant colony, in which the initial impact of actions or events tends to be magnified over time. Its opposite, 'negative feedback', is used to describe systems in which initial effects are dampened and smoothed away. As we shall see later in the book, almost the whole of conventional economic theory can be thought of as describing systems of negative feedback. But in the real world of the economy and society, positive feedback generally rules.

The crucial trail-laying quality of ants led to more subtle theoretical expectations of the proportions which visit each of the sites. The signals left by the creatures mean that the random choices of the first few ants to leave the nest could exercise a decisive influence on the behaviour of the

3

whole colony. If the choice of each ant were purely random each time it left the nest, because of the very large number of ants, there is a probability of almost one – in other words, almost complete certainty – that the proportions will settle down very close to a 50:50 split. But suppose half a dozen ants went out, foraged and returned with food. These then left trails for the next group to follow, and so on. The random choices of a very small number of ants may not divide evenly between the two sites. Our fair coin tossed enough times will lead to an even split, but it is much less likely that a small number of tosses will give an equal number of heads and tails. (So with six tosses, the odds are *against* an even split.) The trails left by the first returning ants have a potential influence on the decisions of those emerging for the first time and, precisely because the random choice of a *small* number can influence the subsequent decisions of the whole group, the eventual proportions visiting the two sites may differ quite markedly from a 50:50 split.

A key feature of the biologists' theory was that the proportions in any given experiment would settle down to the pattern determined in the early stages of the food foraging process. There would be some random fluctuations around this for a short time, but the eventual outcome would be stable.

This theoretical framework is an important one. It predicts that, once a few more ants, for whatever reason, start to visit one of the sites rather than the other there will be a strong tendency for that site to become the favoured destination for more and more ants. Some of the early recruits to the other site might stay loyal, as it were, but we expect an unbalanced outcome to arise. And once this has arisen, the proportions will then remain fixed. Or, in the jargon, the system will stay locked in that particular solution.

In fact, what was seen to take place was a completely different outcome. Even when the experiment had been running for a long time, in ant terms, the proportion of the total ant population visiting any one site continued to fluctuate in an apparently random fashion. The proportions averaged out at one half, but this precise outcome was hardly ever observed, and the proportion was subject to constant change. Once a large majority of ants had visited one of the sites, the outcome tended to stay reasonably stable and exhibited small variations around that

4

proportion for some considerable time. But the majority was always eroded and the ants switched to visiting the other site. Sometimes these shifts were not only very large – from, say, an 80:20 division at one pile to the reverse outcome of 20:80 – but also rapid.

The constant changes, often small but occasionally rapid and large, were entirely unexpected according to the biologists' theory. This conflict between the actual and theoretical outcomes led the experiment to be repeated in different ways. The exact recruitment mechanism which is used varies between species of ants, so different species were tried. The outcome was the same. Doubts then arose as to whether there was some subtle change in the food source which was the cause of the fluctuations, such as the piles not being replenished in an absolutely symmetrical way. So the experiment was tried with just one food source and two identical bridges, precisely the same distance away from the nest, and the proportion going over each of the bridges was observed. Again, the same pattern of behaviour was monitored.

The economist Alan Kirman, then based at the European University Institute in Florence, turned his mind to the problem. By definition, in circumstances such as the ant experiment, the idea that the system as a whole can be understood by the behaviour of a single, representative agent is a complete non-starter. For the overall outcome arises as a result of the interactions between individuals, and the changes in behaviour which they induce in one another. It is, quite literally, impossible to infer the behaviour of the group as a whole from an account of one of its individuals taken in isolation. Kirman has in fact been one of the world leaders in pioneering the development of interacting agent models in economics. But, to paraphrase the words of a popular song, what's ants got to do with it?

Kirman set up a theoretical model which gives an excellent account of the observed behaviour of the seemingly perverse ants. And it can also be stated quite simply. An ant coming out of the nest follows one of three possibilities: it visits the food pile it previously visited; it is persuaded by a returning ant to visit the other source; or, of its own volition, it decides to try the other pile itself. And this is almost all that is required to explain the complex and seemingly baffling phenomenon of the fluctuations in the proportions of ants visiting the respective piles.

I use these simple basic principles throughout the book to explain many social and economic problems. At any point in time an individual agent – whether an ant, a person, a company, or whatever – can follow one of three choices: to stay with its previous decision; to select an alternative of its own accord; or to be persuaded to switch to the alternative by the actions of others.

In such circumstances, no single outcome of an experiment will ever be identical to another, for the choices of individual ants are not fixed, but can be altered each time with given probabilities. This random element to the whole process means that each solution of Kirman's theoretical model, and the outcome of each practical experiment, is unique. But a typical simulation, or outcome, is plotted in Figure 1.1, which shows the proportion of ants visiting one of the food sources at any one time. The chart illustrates the typical patterns of constant small changes and occasional large shifts which are observed.

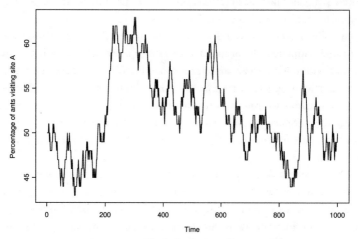

FIGURE 1.1 Typical solution of ants model

When its properties are examined more deeply, such simulated data exhibits characteristics which are entirely typical of situations in which the behaviour of any individual agent is influenced directly by the behaviour of others. In the short term, movements in the series are quite unpredictable. Even with completely accurate knowledge of the equations which describe the behaviour of the individual ants, it is not possible to predict with any degree of accuracy the direction of change of the proportion of ants which visit either of the food sources.

Indeed, in this particular system, non-predictability appears in its most extreme form. We can work out the probability of the very next ant about to collect food visiting a particular site, but we can never do any better than this. In other words, all we can ever say is that the next ant has a certain probability of visiting one site, and a certain probability of visiting the other. In the same way, with the toss of a fair coin, we can never do better than say that there is a probability that a head will appear, and one that a tail will appear. Any 'prediction' can be no better than a pure guess.

One way of looking at this is to see if we can draw any conclusions about the way the system will move from any given split of the colony between the sites. Look, for example, at what happens when the split is 55:45. Reading across from the point marked '55' on the left-hand axis, we can see a number of occasions on which this split occurred in this particular simulation of the model. The first time, the proportion of ants visiting site A then rose rapidly to over 60 per cent. The next time the 55:45 split happened, the proportion visiting this site subsequently fell by a small amount. Moving across to the peak at the far right of the chart, the proportion visiting site A rose by a small amount for a short time. But then, as it fell back through 55 it continued to fall quite sharply. In other words, the proportions we observe at any point in time give us no information about what will happen to the proportions in the immediate future.

But the system does have a very distinct pattern in the longer term. Figure 1.2 sets out for the ants model how much time the system spends at any given distribution of the ant colony between the food sources, whenever the experiment is run for a reasonable length of time. The precise shape of this distribution will vary according to the persuasiveness with which ants can convert others, and on the propensity of individuals to change their own minds.

Figure 1.2 shows the relative amounts of time which a proportion of the ant population spends at each site, when the propensity to switch behaviour is low. The bottom axis of the chart shows the percentage visiting site A, so when the value is close to zero, by implication almost 100 per cent of the ants are visiting site B, and vice versa. The left-hand

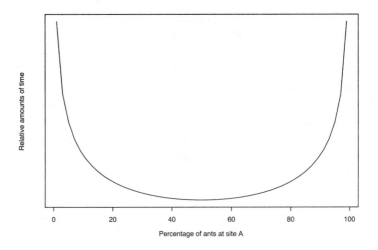

FIGURE 1.2 Relative amounts of time for different percentages of ants at site A,
low propensity to switch behaviour

axis of the chart shows the amount of time a particular proportion of the
ants is observed visiting site A. The U-shape of the curve tells us that the
ants spend much more time at extremes of the split between the two sites
than they do at reasonably equal distributions. In other words, the colony
spends much of its time in situations where either almost every ant visits
site A and very few site B, or almost every ant visits site B and very few
site A. In contrast, the occasions on which a split close to 50:50 is
observed are relatively few and far between.

Figure 1.3 sets out the same kind of plot as Figure 1.2, but one feature
has changed. In this case the propensities of the ants to switch behaviour
are high.

Comparing Figures 1.2 and 1.3, a potential paradox appears to arise. In
the first figure, ants have only a low propensity to change their behaviour
and visit a different site, and in the second they are much more likely to
switch. Yet in Figure 1.2, much more time is spent with most of the ants
visiting either site A or site B than is the case in Figure 1.3, where the ants
spend much more time split closer to 50:50 between the sites.

A first impression might suggest that a high likelihood of changing

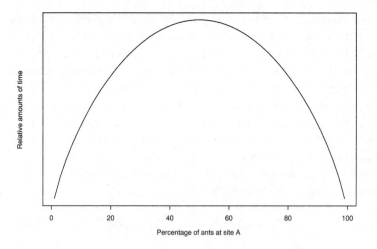

FIGURE 1.3 Relative amounts of time for different percentages of ants at site A, high propensity to switch behaviour

behaviour would drive the system to the extremes, rather than a low one. But in fact, if ants often change the site they visit, the chance of most of them ending up at one or other of the sites is very low, for the very reason that lots of them change their mind each period. In contrast, if changes are only occasional, once the proportion has drifted to an extreme split, it will take a very long time to change. It may take a long time to ever get into such a situation, but once there, the proportion will take even longer to be altered significantly.

The behaviour of individual ants, their direct influence on the behaviour of others, and the consequences of this interaction between individuals for the colony as a whole can be applied as a very general description, or model, of a wide range of economic and social phenomena. For the principles which govern the behaviour of ants also apply to humans. Much of the time, individuals face a limited number of choices in any particular situation. If there are more than two choices, this is just an extension of the fundamental ideas which can be readily incorporated. There are other extensions, complications and simplifications which we will come across in the course of this book as we consider different

9

circumstances and different problems. But the essential principles of the ants model remain. In most circumstances, a person can either stay with the pattern of behaviour he or she previously followed (an ant visiting its previous site), can decide to switch of his or her own volition, or can be influenced into switching by the observed behaviour of others.

The consequences of this description of individual behaviour have, as we shall see, deep implications for the outcome for the human colony as a whole. Many important social and economic issues share the key characteristics of ant behaviour, of unpredictability in the short run merging imperceptibly over time into a form of regularity, of complex systems living at the edge of chaos.

CHAPTER 2

Dedicated Followers of Fashion

The basic concepts involved in the ants model can be observed in many apparently disparate circumstances in the real world. My first two examples, from the restaurant trade and the film industry, may seem rather trivial, even though these areas of economic activity are becoming increasingly significant. But they do illustrate important principles which have far-reaching consequences not just for economics but for the other social sciences. Short-term prediction and control of the overall outcome is either very difficult or impossible, although there may be regularities that appear over time in terms of the proportions of time which the system spends at different outcomes. Even periods of apparent stability are characterized by persistent small changes, punctuated from time to time by large and rapid movements.

Several restaurants are often located very close together in a street. There may be a clear differentiation of their products – such as the nature of the cuisine, price level and so on – or there may be two or three offering very similar food at comparable prices. The custom of these restaurants tends to fluctuate in a seemingly inexplicable way. One month, one will be bursting at the seams, while another will be half empty, only for quite the opposite to be observed the following month. Of course, these particular kinds of food source do differ from those of our ants, in that the proprietors, far from trying to ensure that their sites are identical, will be constantly thinking about ways in which they can improve them and steal a march on their rivals. Yet the fluctuations in custom will often seem unconnected to their marketing efforts. For they are being driven by the same kind of dynamics which determines the outcome of the ants model. Potential customers hear a particular restaurant being praised or damned by their friends and neighbours, and may allow this to influence their choice when they next eat out. In other words, there is a probability that deciding which food source to visit will be influenced by meeting someone else who has visited one of them recently. Further, an individual restaurant-goer, no matter how loyal he or she has been to a particular outlet, may, like our ants, experiment with a different one through his or her own volition.

A substantial degree of uncertainty is therefore inherent in the process of judging, say, how many people will visit a restaurant in the coming week. This creates the same qualitative difficulties for the policy-maker – in this case the restaurant owner – as it does at more elevated levels in the economy. Short-term prediction is hard. And it is difficult to judge the immediate impact of a marketing ploy, for, in the absence of such an initiative, the underlying dynamics of the situation might have been about to deliver a sharp upturn or downturn in the level of bookings. So there is a distinct risk that the wrong conclusions may be drawn about the effect of such policies.

When this chapter was first being written, the film *Anaconda* emerged as an enormous and completely unexpected box office hit in the United States. Described by one film critic as 'a movie about huge snakes devouring a B-grade cast', it nevertheless took $43 million in cinema receipts in the first three weeks of its release. This is by no means untypical in the film industry. Indeed, during the process of revising the chapter, the low-budget British film *The Full Monty*, featuring as its key characters redundant steel workers from a depressed, industrial part of Britain, also became a major American hit. Tremendous successes emerge from nowhere, and films made with huge budgets, replete with glittering names, can flop. Recent examples of major commercial failures include *Hudson Hawk* and *The Postman*, despite massive funding and leading stars.

The American economists Arthur De Vany and W. David Wallis published an article in the *Economic Journal* in November 1996 using a more complicated version of the ants model to account for success or failure in the American cinema. They tested the model by comparing its properties with those of the weekly data provided by *Variety*'s Top 50 films in America. The principle of positive feedback operated with devastating effect. During the nine months which they analysed, the top four films took over 20 per cent of all box office receipts, and the bottom four less than one hundredth of 1 per cent. The highest-grossing film had revenue of $49 million, whereas the film exactly in the middle (defined as the position where the number taking more than its revenue is the same as the number taking less) took only $300,000. And the worst performer had a total revenue of under $5,000, representing a ratio of 10,000:1 in favour of the most successful over the least.

The tremendous uncertainty surrounding the success or failure of a new release is reflected in the very brief tenure of studio heads. De Vany and Wallis attempted to contact nearly 400 film executives, but one third of their letters were simply returned with no forwarding address. A disaster with a major film can even bankrupt a studio, as happened, for example, with United Artists and *Heaven's Gate*.

The key to the whole process is interacting agents. Movie-goers make or break films by telling their friends, an activity which is reinforced by the role of reviewers. The ants leave a trail for others to follow, but here the word is spread through conversation and reading newspapers. In the orthodox economic theory of consumer behaviour, the tastes and preferences of individuals are given, and the individual then acts so as to maximize his or her 'utility' with respect to these tastes. In the film industry, when a new release is issued, consumers do not know in advance whether they will like it or loathe it. In conventional theory, the actions of individuals are held to reveal their true preferences, but here they have to discover what their preferences really are, which is why the opinions of others influence individual behaviour to such a high degree.

The multiplicity of choices available to film-goers leads to an even greater role for the opinions and actions of others in deciding the behaviour of any individual. In the ants model, there are just two food sources from which to choose. In the cinema, any one of the Top 50 films is a potential 'source' to visit. As soon as differences begin to emerge between films, they compound with great speed, hence the enormous differences in revenues earned by the most and least successful.

The scope of the available choice is far, far greater than the simple difference between two and fifty possible destinations. Indeed, for all practical purposes, in the film context, the dimension is infinitely large. One person may be a film fanatic, and religiously view every film in the Top 50. At the other extreme, someone else may see none of them. And it is not just the number of films which an individual sees which counts, but the order in which they are seen. For it is the experience of going to a film which spreads the news to others about its value. Seeing a film on the last day of its release does not have the same potential impact as seeing it on the first. The possible permutations of the number of films seen and the order in which they are seen is, even for an individual, gigantic. De Vany and Wallis point out that in a world of just 1,000 film-goers and fifty cinemas, the number of possible outcomes is more than 10 followed by 210 zeros.

Enormous uncertainty and hence difficulty of prediction is therefore inherent in the film industry. Even the existence of major stars and a huge advertising budget is no guarantee of success. Indeed, the fact that such a film is released at a large number of cinemas compounds the risk. If the initial audiences do not take to it, this information will spread very rapidly, and the studio will be left with a major failure. The uncertainty of the industry is reflected in its structure. For example, contracts between studios and distributors are very flexible and adaptive, containing large numbers of contingency clauses to try to cover the wide range of possible outcomes.

An even more important application, given by Alan Kirman, of the principles of the ants model occurs in the financial markets. Anyone who follows the financial press even in a rather cursory manner is bound to come across a very curious phenomenon. A currency such as the dollar may be widely described as being over-valued. In other words, there is a general perception that, in this instance, the dollar is in some sense too high against other major currencies. Yet foreign exchange traders will continue to buy the dollar in large amounts.

This example is not merely for illustration, for it actually happened on rather a grand scale. In the early 1980s, comments began to circulate that the dollar was over-valued, and the trickle turned into a tidal wave. For most of 1983, the whole of 1984, and into 1985, it was scarcely possible to pick up the *Wall Street Journal* or the *Financial Times* without reading about a stockbroker or dealer expressing this view. Yet, far from selling dollars, which seems the rational thing to do in these circumstances, dealers bought more and more of the currency. The dollar did, of course, eventually crash rather spectacularly in 1985, but for the best part of two years, dealers had exhibited clear signs of schizophrenia. They both knew and said that it was over-valued, yet still they continued to buy.

This kind of behaviour of financial markets is a severe embarrassment for orthodox economic theory. The theory of free markets ought to come closest to reality in exactly the world of exchange rates, shares and bonds. They operate in an almost completely unrestricted way, free of government intervention; information is widely and very rapidly available to all agents in the market; there are a large number of buyers and sellers; markets exist not just to buy and sell today, but contracts can be struck to trade in a variety of complicated ways at dates in the future.

Movements in asset prices – to use the technical term which embraces currencies, equities, government bonds and so on – are explained by economists in terms of the 'efficient markets' hypothesis. This exists in several different guises, each with its own nuance, but it is the general qualities of the theory which are of interest to us here. There are two basic ideas. First, that the price of an asset should reflect its 'fundamentals'. Ownership of a share in a company, for example, brings an entitlement to be paid dividends, and this future stream of dividends represents the underlying, fundamental value of the company. So the price of the share today is supposed to reflect the combined value of all dividends which are expected to be paid in the future. The second key concept is that all information which is available about fundamentals has to both be available to everyone and, through its widespread availability, be incorporated into prices. If it is not, those with the information can exploit it to make profits at the expense of everyone else. If it is the case, then the only reason why prices will change is when new information is made available. And this new information must not have been predictable in any way, because otherwise it would have been worth someone's while to predict it.

In many ways, the efficient markets theory is a reasonable description of how prices on financial markets actually move. The assumption, for example, that prices can only change when new, unpredictable information becomes available, implies that asset prices will move completely randomly over time. If the factor which changes prices is unpredictable, then the changes in prices themselves will be unpredictable, in the same way that the outcome of a random process such as the toss of a fair coin cannot be forecast. An immense literature exists on the question as to whether asset prices are truly random. Certainly, it appears to be extremely difficult to devise trading rules from past information which will make systematic profits in the future.

But the most important empirical difficulty for the efficient markets hypothesis is the fact that movements in asset prices are far too volatile. The range of fluctuations in the share price of a company is typically much greater than that of the stream of dividends which the company actually pays over time. Prices fluctuate much more than do fundamentals. The economist Kenneth Arrow, who won the Nobel Prize and first placed free-market theory on a modern and rigorous mathematical basis, has described this as an 'empirical falsification' of orthodox theory. Or, in plain English, the theory is wrong.

Of course, the efficient markets theory relates to the expectations of future dividends rather than to dividends themselves. So it could be, and is, argued that the theory is correct because the relationship between expectations and fundamentals is markedly non-linear, so small changes in expectations feed through to large changes in prices. But this is not much more than high-class sophistry. Expectations cannot be measured, and so the relationship between them and prices can never be tested in a way which leads to the hypothesis being falsified.

Path-breaking work on the relative volatility of share prices and dividends was carried out in a series of papers in the 1980s by the American economist Robert Shiller. He used American data over more than a century, from 1871 to 1979, to chart the actual value of share prices against the 'true' value which a perfectly rational market ought to have assigned to them on the basis of how dividends actually turned out. The line on the chart representing dividends is very stable, but the share-price line shows tremendous volatility, remaining at extremes of over- or under-valuation for long periods of time.

In any event, as Alan Kirman has remarked, 'it is difficult to believe that there could be a sudden change in the fundamentals which would lead agents simultaneously within half a day to the view that returns in the future had gone down by over 20 per cent. Yet this is what would have to be argued for the October 1987 episode on world stock markets.' In recent years, the Nikkei index of Japanese shares has seen spectacular falls, and it now stands at barely one-third of its peak level.

Further, we often see large and sudden changes in the values of major currencies, as in the example of the US dollar discussed above. After long periods of relative stability, in which agents declare that the currency is over-valued but still buy it, the currency then collapses suddenly. For most of the 1990s, for example, the yen was very strong against the dollar, but then fell in value by some 50 per cent in the space of a year. The East Asian economies were eulogized for years as the strongest in the world, the wave of the future. Yet towards the end of 1997, their currencies collapsed against the US dollar, in some cases losing over 80 per cent of their value in a matter of days.

The actual behaviour of financial asset markets causes difficulties for conventional efficient markets theory, which can be summarized as follows. First, if sharp changes in price are solely due to changes in fundamentals, as the theory requires, why do we not observe equally large fluctuations over time in the fundamentals themselves? Second, if prices change without any obvious change in fundamentals, some operators in the market must be acting irrationally, which is contrary to the basic precepts of the theory.

The theoretical framework provided by the ants model allows us both to account for the volatility of asset prices, and to understand why dealers continue to buy an asset despite believing that it is over-valued compared to the price indicated by the fundamentals.

There is, of course, a risk that readers might become too excited at this point and anticipate that the secret of making risk-free profits is about to be revealed! For those of a nervous disposition, the words of Miss Prism to her young charge Cecily Cardew in Oscar Wilde's play *The Importance of Being Earnest* must be recalled: 'Cecily, you will read your *Political Economy* in my absence. The chapter on the "Fall of the Rupee" you may omit. It is somewhat too sensational.' But, on a more mundane note of reassurance, although the model of interacting agents gives a much deeper understanding of past behaviour in asset markets than does conventional economic theory, one of its strong conclusions is that future changes in prices are essentially unpredictable.

The idea that the behaviour of others can influence an individual's decision in financial markets is by no means new. From time to time throughout history, examples emerge of schemes which draw in more and more people in spectacular fashion, until the whole edifice collapses. The pyramid selling scheme which led to the virtual disintegration of Albania as a country in early 1997 is but the latest illustration. Historical classics of this genre include the Dutch tulip mania of the seventeenth century, when the price of tulip bulbs was bid up to astronomical levels, and the notorious South Sea Bubble in Britain in the early eighteenth century. The only rationale for these events is that people were influenced very powerfully by the behaviour of others. As prices rose ever more steeply, contrary to the precepts of conventional economic theory, more and more people became desperate to buy.

A more mundane illustration of the principle was given by Keynes. In the politically incorrect Britain of the 1930s, beauty competitions were frequently held in the popular press. But the task was not to choose the most beautiful entrant, but to guess which of the entrants would be chosen by most people who cast a vote. Keynes likened behaviour in the financial markets to this same principle. But he was unable to provide a formal rationale for it, and so descriptions of such behaviour remained purely anecdotal.

Kirman gives a model where, instead of two different food sources, we have two types of operator in the financial markets, who look at different kinds of evidence to judge whether to buy or to sell. He provides completely realistic descriptions of these two types of agent. First, fundamentalists, so called not because of the fervour of their beliefs, but simply because they hold that prices are essentially determined by their underlying, fundamental values. Second, chartists, who bear no relation to the great working-class reform movement of that name in England in the 1840s. Chartists in this context believe that charts of the previous movements of the price of a currency or share over time provide evidence about its future behaviour. The techniques they use vary, from almost mystical mutterings about 'head and shoulders' or the rarely observed (but frequently gesticulated) 'left hand extended V' patterns on a plot of data, to the most advanced rocket science mathematics. But they form a view of future prices by extrapolating from past movements.

These two approaches to prices will often give quite different opinions about what the price of any given asset ought to be. In 1984, a fundamentalist thought that a sharp fall in the dollar ought to take place. But a chartist expected it to stay high, simply because it had been high in the recent past.

The essence of Kirman's model is that in any given period an agent can continue to behave in the same way as before; he or she can change behaviour independently in reaction to news; or the agent can be persuaded to switch by the behaviour of others – by the trails which they leave when their buy or sell decisions appear on the dealing screens. In other words, we have the identical analytical framework to that of the ants model.

As with the ants model, the split between the number of dealers in any given asset who are either fundamentalists or chartists will change continuously. Sometimes almost everyone will be a chartist, but a switch back to the complete opposite at some point is inevitable. The very nature of the dynamics of the process dictates that some of these large changes will be very rapid. And, at these times, we are likely to see a large change in the price of the relevant asset, as it switches from being determined by fundamentals, say, to being generated by extrapolation of its own past behaviour as chartists come to dominate this particular market. In short, asset prices will be volatile because of the underlying volatility of the proportion of different types of agent operating in the market. This is reinforced by the speed with which information is made available and exchanged in financial markets, so there is a very large number of 'meetings' with other agents. It is not a matter of lurking outside the nest waiting for a signal from a returning ant. Information on the activities of others bombards the dealer continuously.

So, in the unexpected setting of Wall Street and Masters of the Universe, our model of ant behaviour provides a better explanation of events than does conventional economic theory. Both imply that changes in asset prices are essentially unpredictable, which appears to be true. But orthodox economics cannot account for the sheer volatility of asset markets, and the paradoxes which arise, such as traders continuing to buy assets which they say are over-valued.

An even more difficult issue for conventional theory arises in the choice and selection of products in areas of new technology. In orthodox economic theory, the consumer is sovereign. He or she has access to all the relevant information, processes it efficiently, and chooses accordingly.

But there are many examples of products which are technologically inferior not just surviving, but driving out of existence competitors with distinctly superior qualities. The free market chooses not the best, but the worst.

An example from the early 1980s is the struggle over the VCR market between Betamax and VHS. Betamax machines were easier to operate and had a number of features which even now are not available in the standard model of VCR. After diligently reading the relevant consumer magazines to discover this information, and behaving exactly in the way free-market theory prescribed, for old habits die hard, I bought one. The purchase was very satisfactory, except for one thing. Within a couple of years, Betamax had been driven out of business by its technologically inferior rival. It became impossible even to buy new Betamax video tapes, although, at least initially, I had some success in obtaining second-hand ones at auctions of the contents of grand country houses enforced by the sharp British recession of the early 1990s. Finally, I had no choice but to bow to majority opinion and purchase a VHS machine.

A longer-lasting illustration, so deeply embedded in our culture that it is scarcely ever noticed, is the design of the QWERTY keyboard. A controversy exists as to whether, in the final decades of the nineteenth century, it was deliberately designed to be inefficient. But, certainly, at various times during the last century, more efficient designs have been invented and marketed, but all have failed. The inferior technology prevails.

The North American economists Robin Cowan and Philip Gunby provide a detailed illustration of pest-control strategies, in the *Economic Journal* of May 1996. In the United States, the use of chemical pesticides remains by far the dominant method of control, even though scientists have warned of its dangers for over thirty years. The alternative which has been developed is integrated pest management, or IPM, which relies upon understanding and enhancing natural controls on species which cause damage. There is a high fixed cost in setting this technology up, but thereafter it is extremely cheap, for it relies on knowledge. And once produced, knowledge is easy to replicate. There have been many studies of the economics of IPM and, at worst, farmers using this strategy rather than chemical control obtain similar profits and rates of return on their investment. At best, they can gain, with one study finding an increase of average returns of $15,000 a year for those farmers using IPM. Cowan and Gunby discuss at length the citrus fruit industry in Israel and cotton in Texas, concluding that IPM is unequivocally superior. Nevertheless, pesticides prevail.

But the phenomenon of one particular offer driving another out of the market, regardless of its initial merits, is not confined to products, whether aimed at consumers or at the industrial market. The location of industry itself often exhibits these features. There may be some objective reasons why Silicon Valley became a favoured location for computer companies, but they can hardly be so strong as to account for the position of dominance which it has achieved. Success often breeds success, and once firms started to locate in Silicon Valley, it became more attractive to others who needed access to the highly skilled labour force being built up in the area. But, in advance of this process getting under way, the region was simply one of a number of potential locations where the computer industry might have started to expand.

Conventional thought on the location of industry places much emphasis on factors such as transport infrastructure to facilitate ease of access. But while many parts of old industrial Britain are closely connected to the motorway network, it is south-east Wales and the north-east of England which show by far the most signs of industrial regeneration, attracting foreign companies in increasing numbers. Areas such as Merseyside, which by objective criteria might appear to be more favourably placed, continue their spiral of decline. This is emphatically not to say that rational reasons can never be given for the concentration of industries in certain locations, or, indeed, that all industries exhibit the same degree of concentration. But geographical clusters of firms do frequently form which are much denser than conventional criteria would lead us to expect.

The key to understanding these phenomena was provided by a deep article published in 1983 by the British polymath Brian Arthur, written jointly with two Russian mathematicians. The title, 'A Generalized Urn Problem and Its Applications', gives no clue that its contents are related to the problems discussed above, but in many ways it is the seminal article on the concept of interacting agents in economic and social theory. It essentially sets out a view of behaviour which is similar to that of our ants model. There are some important differences, but in one sense we can think of Arthur's approach as a simplified version of the ants.

Arthur and his colleagues produced elegant solutions to some difficult issues in probability theory. The questions themselves can be stated quite simply. An urn contains a mixture of white and black balls. A random sample of balls is removed from the urn, and various rules exist about the collection of balls which is put back in. For example, if more than half * the balls removed turn out to be white, the whole sample is returned to the urn, along with an additional white ball. If more than half are black, the sample plus an extra black ball are put back. What, if anything, can we say about the proportion of white to black balls which will emerge in the urn in the long run?

Arthur and his colleagues said a great deal about this, and about other rules for replacement which might be used instead. And Arthur realized that his theorems had direct implications for the choice between competing new technologies for both consumers and firms. A new product is invented, the video recorder, for example, and two competing versions are marketed. Initially, consumers have very little information to guide them about the rival offers. They did not realize previously that such products existed, so their tastes are quite unformed. Indeed, as with our movie example, people have to learn what their preferences are. Suppose, for there is no reason to do otherwise, that the population of potential adopters is divided equally in its preferences between the two. One group is more likely to choose one technology, and the other group its competitor.

The key assumption now is that as more people choose one rather than the other, it becomes increasingly likely that others will subsequently choose the successful version of the product. The choice of version by any agent alters the probability that all subsequent agents will choose this rather than its rival, so that positive feedback takes place. In other words, we have a version of the ants model in which the behaviour of individuals directly alters the behaviour of others.

---

* In this example of a rule, the random sample is always of an odd rather than an even number of balls.

It is easy to think of reasons why people should behave in this way. For example, lacking information, it makes sense to observe what others do and follow their example. If a friend or neighbour buys a VHS machine and is satisfied, you are more likely to do the same. Once this process gets under way, the lead in market share which VHS obtains encourages retailers, for example, to stock tapes for these machines rather than for its rival Betamax, which in turn gives an incentive for new purchasers to choose a VHS machine, so that a virtuous circle comes into existence for VHS, which becomes a vicious one for Betamax.

In terms of Brian Arthur's urn, we can think of a random sample of just one ball being drawn. Suppose it is white, and we put it back in along with another white, according to our rule. After this is done, the proportion of white balls relative to black has risen, if only by a tiny amount. So the probability of drawing a white in the next random sample of one has increased. In terms of two rival new products, the choice of one of them by a consumer shifts the chances, ever so slightly, in favour of the next person making the same choice.

Arthur and his co-authors proved as a theorem that in such circumstances, no matter how small the change in the probabilities following each individual adoption, one technology will eventually gain 100 per cent market share and its rival will be eliminated. By changing the rules on replacement, results are obtained which predict the dominance of one product over the other, but do not require its complete elimination. But this simply stated theory shows why, once we allow for interaction between agents and positive feedback, inferior technologies can drive better ones out of existence, in complete contradiction to the predictions of orthodox consumer theory.

There are two main differences between this model and the one we use to describe the behaviour of our ants.* The first is that the total number of ants in the colony is assumed to be fixed. Of course, in practice there will be births and deaths and the population will change. But it will do so only slowly, if at all, and so analytically it simplifies matters if we think of

---

* There is a third, more subtle one regarding how many agents influence the choice of any individual. In the ants model, only the small number the ant meets on emerging from the nest matter, while in the urn, the *total* split is the factor which alters behaviour. It is as if each ant could observe the overall behaviour of the colony.

the population as being constant. In contrast, the Arthur model relies upon an unlimited supply, or at least a very large number, of new balls being made available. But the second difference is the reason why we might think of the Arthur model, for all its profundity, as a simplification of our ants. Once a ball has been drawn, the consequences for the split between colours – and its impact on the subsequent behaviour of others – is fixed. It is as if once an ant has decided which site to visit, for whatever reason, it never changes its mind again, but is condemned in perpetuity to revisit the same site.

In our ants model, of course, any individual ant can in theory change its mind time after time. Why, then, bother with Arthur's simplified analogy of ant behaviour? The reason is that, in certain circumstances, the assumption that once a decision is taken it cannot then be altered is a good approximation to reality. The simplified version offers a good description of the real world.

Once a firm has a built a plant in Silicon Valley, the Île de France, the Thames Valley, Bavaria or wherever, the decision is very difficult to reverse. It is hardly likely that the buildings will be dismantled brick by brick and shipped across the world.* Similarly, individual consumers who buy an expensive item – and videos were very expensive in their early years – will be very reluctant to change their minds and buy a competing version as well. Eventually, of course, the old product wears out, or they can no longer buy supporting equipment such as video tapes, so they will be forced to do so. But in the short term, we can think of their choice as being effectively fixed.

A nice property of Arthur's model, which reflects what we have already learned about interacting agents, is that it is not possible to predict in advance which technology will succeed: by construction the outcome is determined by the random process of initial adoption. Whoever gains an early lead will set up the process of self-reinforcement, and will probably obtain control of the entire market.

Brian Arthur's theory has come to be known as the theory of QWERTY. It has sparked an important policy debate between economists

---

* Though this did once happen to the old London Bridge, allegedly purchased by Texans who believed they were buying the world famous Tower Bridge rather than its nondescript downriver counterpart.

such as Paul Krugman and policy entrepreneurs like Lester Thurow and Robert Reich. The immediate point at issue between Krugman and his fellow Americans is whether this theory gives a new and powerful justification for state intervention in the economy, both in general and in particular through industrial policy. Admittedly, Reich and Thurow show little awareness of the existence of such theory, especially the mathematical aspects of it – a fact which Krugman is often keen to highlight. But this is merely a debating point. Reich and Thurow – the 'strategic traders' as Krugman calls them – advocate interventionist industrial policy, and whether they can follow the mathematics which in theory offers support for such a stance is irrelevant.

Krugman is very cautious about making policy pronouncements based on this new theory. This is for two reasons. First, he regards acknowledgement of the power and effectiveness of markets as a central part of the identity of professional economists, who should be reluctant to 'come out too brashly against markets having their own way, especially when it comes to the almost sacred principle of free trade'. Second, and more important, he fears that the theory might simply be used to rationalize bad policies.

On the first point, Krugman might have reflected upon the economic history of his own country, particularly during the second half of the nineteenth century when the foundations of its world dominance were being established. Undoubtedly, the sheer resourcefulness and unbounded optimism of many Americans, which continue to the present day, were important factors. But central government played an essential role in the whole process. For example, beginning with the Morrill Tariff of 1861, a series of Acts until 1897 increased sharply the degree of protection which domestic producers in the United States enjoyed. As the Western territories expanded, America became by far the largest domestic market in the world, sheltered behind tariff barriers. Aware of the potential shortage of labour which might arise as the West was opened up, the federal government defended the interests of northern industry by maintaining open doors to immigrants. Further, enormous grants were made from the public purse to the private railway companies.

In short, in common with virtually every country which has ever industrialized successfully, America did so with policies which were in direct contradiction of the theorems of competitive markets and of pure free trade. The Far Eastern economies are but the latest additions to this list.

It can, of course, be argued that such examples merely show that, *ex post facto*, certain forms of intervention and restrictions on trade appear to have been successful. Their existence does not imply *ex ante* that any such policies will necessarily succeed. Logically, this argument is correct. But the theory of QWERTY enables us to set down a few guidelines for the conduct of interventionist industrial strategy, albeit of a different kind from the traditional ones.

For example, support for companies to get new technologies or new products to market as rapidly as possible seems to be a sensible strategy in those industries where early success might secure a decisive advantage. It is a necessary and not sufficient condition for industrial success, but the traditional British Treasury attitude, reflected in finance ministries around the world, of opposing such support as a matter of principle is simply wrong.

A second policy guideline is the encouragement of strategic alliances at, say, the national or European level. An explicit aim of such a framework is to increase the effective degree of monopoly to allow the profit share in national income to rise. The current obsession with consumerism – and preventing companies making high profits through such behaviour – is highly damaging to European industries. Of course, such alliances do need monitoring, to make sure that the profits are being used positively and not simply handed out in dividends. But they are essential in a number of industries to gain the full advantages of increasing returns to scale.

As a final point, the theory suggests very strongly that it is not sensible to support industries where other countries already have a lead. They will already be benefiting from increasing returns in such industries. So, for example, it is misguided to continue to give large subsidies to Air France, Alitalia or Iberian Airways (in the guise of 'restructuring funds' to satisfy European Commission guidelines) in the belief that the companies will be able to establish themselves on the same scale as British Airways, their chief rival.

It is possible, with care and thought, to interfere with market mechanisms in a positive way, and QWERTY provides a rigorous theoretical basis for this intervention. But as Krugman rightly warns, the approach does not give *carte blanche* for any form of intervention which happens to take the political fancy.

The ability to develop models in which the behaviour of individuals is directly affected by the behaviour of others, exemplified by our ants, represents a very important intellectual advance for the social sciences, and offers a more powerful explanation of a wide range of phenomena than does conventional thinking. The message of this approach is by no means easy for policy-makers to digest. Short-term prediction and control, on which so much of public policy is based, is inherently extremely difficult and sometimes literally impossible. A more studied, less frenzied approach is needed, looking at the longer-term properties of the system as a whole, if any real and consistent success is to be achieved.

CHAPTER 3

To Catch a Thief

Margaret Thatcher famously declared, 'There is no such thing as society.' Her intent was ideological rather than intellectual, to assert the primacy of the interests of the individual over that of the state. Our emphasis on the concept of interacting agents, exemplified in our ants, does not in any way lead to a presumption that the interests of society as a whole should be favoured at the expense of the individual. Neither does it imply that the collective outcome is necessarily a desirable one. These remain a matter of personal and political preference.

But it does mean that, in an important sense, there *is* such a thing as society. Analytically, once the principle that the behaviour of individuals can be affected directly by the behaviour of others is accepted, the properties and features of the collective whole can no longer be deduced simply from the conduct of a typical individual. The outcome for the colony in its entirety will not be the same as it would be if it consisted of a single individual operating in complete isolation on a desert island.

In short, the assembled beast behaves differently from its myriad individual component cells, a concept articulated several millennia ago in the book of the prophet Ezekiel: 'son of man, can these bones live?' Or, as the popular song puts it more graphically, 'dem bones, dem bones, dem dry bones'.

The principle of interacting agents, of our ants, ought to be able to illuminate not just economic issues, but questions in the social sciences. The discipline of sociology is, after all, meant to involve the study of society.

A light-hearted, but nevertheless serious, example might be the best way to proceed. The so-called discipline of psephology, the study and prediction of voters' behaviour, is one of the few which is able to make economic forecasting look respectable. Enormous errors in the prediction of election results can be made by experts only days before the actual event, and even on the day itself.

From time to time, a conventional wisdom emerges about what determines the outcome of elections, only for it to be rapidly contradicted by events. Bill Clinton declared that 'it's the economy, stupid', and many psephologists took these words to heart in thinking about the outcome of the British election in 1997. The economy was growing rapidly, unemployment was falling sharply, and inflation was lower than it had been for over thirty years. Yet the ruling Conservatives suffered one of the biggest defeats in their entire history, which stretches back over two hundred years.

The behaviour of Western electorates seems to have two striking features. In terms of the overall division of votes between the leading political parties, there can be long periods of reasonable stability, punctuated by large and rapid changes. The changes in some European countries during the course of this century have been truly dramatic, but the point can be illustrated even in the generally more stable climate of the United Kingdom.

The Liberal Party won an enormous victory in the election of 1906, but were almost defeated in 1910, and by the early 1920s had been reduced to the status of a small minority party, where they have remained ever since. The massive Labour victory of 1945, overthrowing Winston Churchill, was overturned by 1951 and the Conservatives were brought back to power. A large Conservative victory in 1959 had been changed into an equally large Labour one by 1966. Yet there have also been periods of stability with, for example, the Conservatives remaining in power between 1951 and 1964, and again from 1979 to 1997.

The second point relates to evidence at the level of the individual voter. Even when the overall share of votes in opinion polls is reasonably stable, studies which follow the views of the same panel of voters over time indicate a fairly high level of change by individuals. By definition, if the aggregate share of votes is stable, the various changes of mind by individuals must cancel each other out. But these changes of opinion by individuals most definitely exist, even at times of stability in the overall outcome. Psephologists even have their own word to describe such behaviour, the faintly unsettling 'churning'.

In the scientific spirit, we are searching for a model of individual voter behaviour which is compatible with these two pieces of empirical evidence. A steady incidence of switching opinion by individuals, and an overall pattern of voting for the major parties in which periods of stability are followed by swift and substantial changes.

As a first approximation, we need look no further than our friends the ants. To simplify the exposition, imagine that there are only two parties, A and B, and that voting is compulsory, on pain of a penalty so huge and Draconian that everyone does actually vote (it could be, for example, a life sentence condemning non-voters to listen to every single debate which takes place in the national parliament). The model can readily be extended to incorporate more parties, including a nominal one to represent those who choose not to vote at all. But it is easier to start with just two.

An individual who supports party A in any given period of time can, in the next period, do one of three things. He or she can simply continue to support A. The voter may be persuaded, of his or her own volition, or by some piece of news, to switch to party B. We do not need to specify the nature of the news, which we assume arrives at random. Both anecdotal and more structured evidence suggests that voters can and do make up their minds on the most bizarre grounds. For example, I was told in the early 1990s in all seriousness that someone had decided to abandon the Conservatives on the grounds that the then finance minister 'looked like an owl'. Finally, someone may decide to switch as a result of being influenced by the views and decisions of others, such as friends or colleagues at work.

This is exactly the model of ant behaviour. An individual can continue to be loyal to the same party, can decide to switch with a given probability on his or her own account, or can change opinion, with a different probability, as a result of being influenced by others. So the model involves, inherently, a constant stream of changes of opinion by individuals. And, as we saw in the previous chapter, this generates in aggregate the type of behaviour which is actually observed. Periods of relative stability in the division of support between the two parties are interspersed with sharp and rapid changes.

A typical solution of such a model of voting behaviour in a two-party system is plotted in Figure 3.1. The fluctuations over time are not identical to those of Figure 1.1, which plots the proportion of the ant colony visiting one of the food sites, for each solution of the model is unique. But qualitatively, the behaviour is identical.

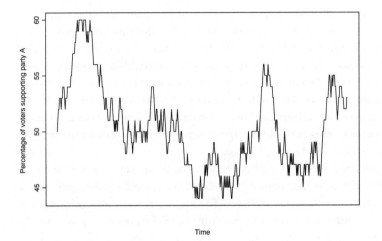

Time

FIGURE 3.1 Voters in a two-party system: typical percentage supporting party A

Notice in the chart that the proportions never get too far away from a 50:50 split. At the national level, this seems to fit with the evidence of what actually happens in two-party systems. Thinking back to Chapter 1, this sort of outcome obtains whenever the individual agents, whether ants or voters, have quite a high probability of changing their minds. Otherwise, the system will at some stage drift towards an extreme split and, once there, be very difficult to move if individuals only switch occasionally. In terms of national voting behaviour or intentions, this is again consistent with the evidence from pollsters: against a background of overall relatively stability, there is a great deal of 'churning' at the individual level.

In more local areas, we often observe, in contrast, very long periods of domination by a single party, whether Democrat or Republican, Labour or Conservative, or whatever. Again, this is compatible with the evidence that certain areas of a country are known to have concentrations of traditional supporters of one particular party, with low propensities to change their minds.

But a number of refinements are desirable if the ants model is applied to voting behaviour. To assume, for example, that all voters have the same probability of switching parties in a given period is obviously not an accurate description of reality. Some voters are life-long Democrats, Republicans or whatever, and the chances that they will change their minds are very small. Others are far more fickle, and in consequence are the focus of a great deal of attention from the political parties, whose marketing efforts are concentrated on this group of so-called floating voters.

This can be dealt with in a fairly straightforward, albeit technical, manner. The simplifying assumption that all voters share the same probability of change is equivalent to taking the average of a wide range of individual probabilities. Equally, it is not difficult to let individual agents in the model have their own probability of switching allegiance, and to simulate the model accordingly. The results are essentially very similar to those we get with our simple postulate that everyone is equally likely to change.

The real limitation of the approach as it stands is that it admits no possibility of analysing the effects of factors which are thought to have a systematic influence on voter behaviour. The understanding of these may well be imperfect, as the example of the British economy in 1997 shows, but political parties devote an increasing amount of effort, using sophisticated marketing techniques developed in the fast-moving consumer goods markets, to try to influence the outcome.

Certainly, in many consumer markets, companies are often able to implement strategies which successfully increase their market share over that of their main competitor(s). Typically, the strategy will be effective for only a limited period of time, not least because rivals will respond to a successful attack on their sales. But it is important to be able to incorporate such effects more readily into the analysis.

A very practical illustration is given by the topic of crime. I first became curious about the literature on crime several years ago, during the British election campaign of 1992. I turned to the BBC teletext pages to see the headlines: 'Page 101, Mrs Thatcher to be allowed to play key role in Tory campaign'; 'Page 102, battle-axe murder woman set free'. I paid quiet tribute to the flash of brilliance with which the unknown sub-editor had juxtaposed these two stories, and then reflected on the specific question raised implicitly by the latter: does prison work?

After brooding on and off about the question for a few years, my thoughts were stimulated by the thirtieth anniversary lecture of the British National Association for the Care and Rehabilitation of Offenders (NACRO) given in 1996 by the leading American liberal criminologist Elliott Currie. In his NACRO lecture, Currie drew an analogy between the spread of an epidemic and the growth in crime. His specific purpose in so doing was to offer a criticism of the American emphasis on incarceration, using the analogy that a health policy of putting all those who were ill in hospital would not be regarded as a particularly successful solution to the problem. Instead, the focus would be on preventing people from getting the disease in the first place.

The analysis of the processes by which diseases spread is conceptually quite distinct from the medical understanding of their specific causes and cures. Obviously in practice the two are related; for example, the discovery of a new vaccination will influence the spread of the particular disease it is designed to combat. But, for any given state of medical knowledge, it is important to have an understanding of whether a particular disease can be contained or whether it will break out into an epidemic. On a parochial note, Britain is one of the few countries in which the fatal disease of rabies is not endemic. An efficient carrier of the rabies virus is the fox population, and biologists have analysed the conditions under which rabies might spread, and how rapidly it would do so, in the United Kingdom. More dramatically, predicting the spread of AIDS is of crucial importance to many governments and societies around the world.

The techniques developed by biologists for analysing these questions are highly mathematical, but rest upon a simple proposition, namely that the spread or otherwise of a disease is fundamentally a social process. It moves from person to person, or animal to animal, by social interaction. The common cold is caught in a variety of ways, but only by being in close proximity to someone who already has it. HIV is disseminated by being in even closer proximity. This concept of the spread of infections as a social process is based on exactly the same principle of interacting agents as our ants model, where the behaviour of individuals is influenced directly by the behaviour of others. In the biological models, individual behaviour is influenced in the very specific sense of catching a disease from someone else.

In the context of the ants model, the greater the proportion of the colony which is already visiting a particular site, the higher the chances of meeting ants who have just been there, and so the more likely it is that any given individual will forage at the same site. In Arthur's urns in the previous chapter, the more black balls the urn already contains, the greater the chances that another black one will be chosen. And in the biological models, the larger the proportion of any given population who are infected with a disease, the higher the probability that any individual will catch it.

These disparate examples are linked analytically by the same under-lying principle: what happens to other agents in the system – be they ants, balls or people – can influence directly what any given agent will do.

The techniques used by biologists to understand the spread of disease can be applied to analysing crime, precisely because we can regard crime as being in part a social process. So, the more criminals there are in a given population, the higher the probability that any particular individual will also decide to be a criminal.

Before moving on to develop this approach, it is important to reflect on the large, conventional literature which already exists on economics and crime. If this gave us a good understanding of what caused crime and therefore how we could reduce it, there would be little point in constructing a different analytical approach to the problem. But despite voluminous research over at least thirty years, no firm conclusions have emerged from the orthodox economic approach.

Crime and the fear of crime have become major concerns of the electorates of many Western countries, and especially so in Britain and the United States. In the atmosphere of almost permanent electioneering which now exists, it is understandable that the main political parties are terrified of appearing to be soft on this issue. Admittedly, no one in the United Kingdom has yet gone as far as Bill Clinton in the 1992 American election campaign, when, as Governor of Arkansas, he refused clemency in a very public way and allowed at least one dubious execution to proceed. But the whole tenor of political debate in Britain and elsewhere is moving in the direction of controls, sanctions and penalties.

It is easy to see why this is attractive to policy-makers. Crime statistics are notoriously unreliable, but there clearly has been a big rise in crime over the past thirty years or so. And, just as clearly, the costs of crime are borne disproportionately by the poorer groups in society. In pre-war days, the poor were alleged to make a living by taking in each other's washing. On some housing estates today, it is almost as if they exist by committing crimes against one another.

The United States has intensified the punitive aspect of the criminal justice system in the past twenty years or so, and during the 1990s, according to a wide range of measures, crime rates have fallen. Prison appears to work. But Elliott Currie was not alone when he raised serious questions about this strategy in his 1996 NACRO lecture. Currie points out that in 1970 there were just under 200,000 inmates in American state and federal prisons. Today, the figure is around 1 million – a five-fold increase. He recognizes that this has had some effect in reducing crime. But crime rates today, as a broad generalization, are still high in comparison to the 1950s and 1960s.

There is a crucial, and so far unresolved, debate about whether the costs of such a policy outweigh the benefits. The expense involved in building and maintaining the necessary number of prisons is, of course, enormous. But, it is argued, the benefits of preventing crime are also large. Crime imposes costs, and so reducing crime brings a benefit to society. But, as Currie argues, the real debate should be about which approach to the control of crime works best. Could the huge amounts spent on the American prison system be more effective if they were used instead on strategies of crime prevention? The enormous conventional literature which exists on this, and other, questions, is almost wholly inconclusive.

Economists are notorious among social scientists for their intellectual imperialism. Not content with thinking about the economy, in the last two decades their minds have turned to a wide range of social phenomena, such as the family and the decision to have children, and also to crime. Economic analysis of the phenomenon of crime was stimulated in the late

1960s by the distinguished Chicago economist and subsequent Nobel prizewinner Gary Becker, and a vast amount has since been written.

In orthodox economic theory, the agents involved in any particular market, whether consumers or producers, are assumed to act in accordance with the rules of what is called maximizing behaviour. They are presumed to be able to both gather and process substantial amounts of information efficiently in order to form expectations on the likely costs and benefits associated with different courses of action, and to respond to incentives and disincentives in an appropriate manner. In other words, an individual is deemed to behave in a way which maximizes his or her 'utility'.

The one thing these hypothetical individuals do *not* do, it should be said, is to allow their behaviour to be influenced directly by the behaviour of others. For agents in economic models are very dogmatic, and their tastes and preferences are assumed to be fixed, regardless of how others behave.

According to this standard economic view of the world, crime can be thought of as a market, just like the market for baked beans. This does not, of course, imply that there is a physical setting, such as the supermarket, in which crime is traded – people cannot go out and put a can of bank robberies in their trolley and pay for it at the till. But it does mean that the behaviour of those involved in crime, whether criminals, law enforcers, purchasers of stolen goods or victims, is co-ordinated through adjustments in relative prices, through the perception of the likely benefits compared to the likely costs.

The decision whether or not to participate in crime is made, coolly and rationally, by weighing up the costs and benefits. The benefit is obviously the gains from the proceeds of crime, while the costs include the actual costs incurred in carrying out a crime (such as the purchase of a crowbar by a burglar), the probability of being caught, and the prospective penalty if convicted. In this model, punishment by the criminal justice system can be thought of as a tax on the supply of crime, which increases the cost and hence reduces the amount which is supplied.

This view of crime as the outcome of a rational assessment by individuals of the relative costs and benefits involved is in marked contrast to the tenets of conventional criminology, which portrays the typical criminal as having difficulty identifying and assessing alternative courses of action, rarely thinking through the consequences of actions, and not thinking about possible punishments.

This basic divergence between how conventional economics and criminology view individuals' behaviour is at the root of many of the disagreements on policy. The probability of, and severity of, a prison sentence will have little effect in deterring many potential criminals according to the criminological view of behaviour, whereas for the economist its theoretical impact is taken for granted, and the question is then simply an empirical one of how strong it is in practice.

But finding a consensus in the vast applied literature on the impact of different factors on crime is very difficult. Even the research carried out within the common framework of orthodox economic theory reaches few clear policy conclusions on crime. Isaac Ehrlich was one of the first economists to take up the theme launched by Becker, and in 1996 he published an excellent exposition of this approach to crime which discusses much of the empirical literature. Ehrlich remarks that, despite the 'voluminous' nature of this literature, on the crucial question of the impact of incentives on crime, 'it would be premature to view the empirical evidence as conclusive'.

He notes that the quantitative estimates of such effects vary, even to the extent of a minority of studies failing to find any effect at all. The point which is of most concern to Ehrlich is that the empirical evidence gives no real guide as to whether negative or positive incentives exert the more influence over crime. But this distinction is at the very heart of the policy debate. 'Negative' incentives are those which deter and prevent crime – the probability and severity of punishment. 'Positive' incentives are those which encourage people to take up legitimate work instead of crime, such as the probability of obtaining a job at a decent wage, rehabilitation programmes, and policies which help to provide strong, non-criminal role models for those individuals who are most susceptible to commit crime.

In short, the conventional economic approach based upon statistical analysis of actual data has made very little progress in our understanding of crime. Alternatives *are* needed.

The aim of our approach is to give a *general* description of the process by which people become criminals. Conceptually, the population –

whether that of an entire country, a local neighbourhood, a particular age group, or whatever – is divided at any one time into a small number of discrete groups which differ in their potential to commit crime. In other words, an individual at any point is in one or other state, defined by the propensity to carry out criminal acts.

In its most basic form, we can think of the population as being divided into three groups. First, those who are not susceptible to commit a crime (group N, for 'not susceptible'). In other words, individuals with a zero probability of committing a crime. A reasonable approximation might place most groups of women, certainly those over twenty-five, in this category, as well as most pensioners.

The second group is made up of the susceptibles (S), those who have not committed a crime, but might well do so. It is very well documented in the criminology literature that young men in their teens and early twenties are particularly prone to commit crimes. Of course, by no means all men in this age group actually commit crimes, but there is a high propensity to do so – from acts of minor vandalism carried out in what used to be known as 'high spirits', to brawling in public, to far more serious crimes. For instance, the rather disagreeable youths portrayed in the film *Trainspotting* show a remarkably high propensity to convert from being merely susceptible to being criminals.

The third group is made up of those who are active criminals (C). These three groups, N, S and C by definition make up the whole population. The approach can be extended and made more complicated, by splitting the C group into occasional and habitual criminals, by introducing a category for those in prison at any time, and so on, but the essential dynamics of the system can be understood by analysis of the simpler version.

The key ingredient of the approach is to describe the flows between these groups, the overall effect of which describes the evolution of crime rates. Of course, modelling the proportion of any given population in the criminal category does not necessarily describe the evolution of crime rates over time. In some areas, such as vehicle crime, the increase in opportunity afforded by the spread of car ownership has led to the typical car criminal committing many more offences per unit of time. But a description of how the number of crimes committed by each criminal evolves over time could easily be added to the model to give this information. Our concern is to describe the processes which determine the proportion of the population who are in the criminal category at any point.

There are undoubtedly many factors which govern both membership of and movement between the various categories over time. Some will be of lasting influence, and some will be ephemeral. The aim of the model is to synthesize the key elements which give rise to changes in the relative size of these groups over time. I assume that the flows between these groups depend upon factors such as demographics, the impact of negative incentives such as the deterrent effects of the criminal justice system, and general social and economic conditions. The orthodox empirical literature on crime does identify such factors as being of potential importance, although the literature gives widely differing views of their actual importance.

The essential part of the model, which gives it entirely different properties from the conventional economic approach, is the influence of social interaction on the behaviour of agents. For any given set of external determinants of crime, the bigger the proportion of the population in any given category, the more likely it is that individuals in other categories will switch into that one. In other words, we incorporate the basic principle of the behaviour of our ants into our approach to crime.

Social interaction is introduced in our model in two ways. First, the greater the proportion of people in any given population who are already criminals, the more likely it is that any other individual will convert to becoming a criminal. Second, the greater the proportion of the population who are wholly uninterested in being criminals, the greater the pressure on those who are criminals to become law-abiding.

In short, in our simplified model, individuals are assumed to form views on external factors, such as the overall social and economic conditions and the punishment structure, and to use these to determine their movement or otherwise in or out of the different categories in the model. No presumption is made that they do so in an economically 'rational' way. But in addition, the essential element in this approach, as in our ants model, is that the behaviour of individuals can be altered by the behaviour of others. This social interaction between individual agents is crucial to the process of how crime rates evolve over time.

So far, this may all seem rather abstract. But a good test of the credibility of the approach is how it accounts for by far the most important fact about crime rates – their enormous variability across time and place. Even making due allowance for problems with the reliability of the data, there are massive variations, even at the level of individual housing estates which are virtually next door to each other.

These variations are too large to be accounted for by differences in factors such as unemployment and the nature of the punishment system. Indeed, such factors often appear to have perverse effects in the conventional literature. A highly topical instance, which is frequently invoked in the current policy debate in Britain, is the contrast between crime rates in the 1930s and crime rates today. Unemployment and poverty are cited by liberal criminologists as being important in explaining the current high rates of crime. Conservatives counter this by pointing to the example of the 1930s when these possible determinants were much more acute, yet according to both official data and the testimonies of those alive at the time, crime was much lower than it is today.

A more general example of this phenomenon is the wide variations in crime rates between the rural and urban sectors of poor economies; crime is often much lower in the poor rural areas than in the richer, urban ones. Elliott Currie attributes the low rates in the rural areas mainly to the community relationships, which both foster a sense of belonging and provide 'the setting in which informal social sanctions against aggression and crime can operate effectively'. Criminologists, if not economists, speak the language of our ants: the behaviour of others can directly influence the behaviour of any particular individual.

Our biological approach is intended to offer a general description of the process by which crime rates evolve. Its plausibility depends on it being able to produce outcomes in which crime rates differ substantially, whether over time in a particular population or comparing different populations at a point in time, without having to rely upon large differences in factors such as social and economic conditions and the negative incentives of the justice system. Further, it must also be able to generate seemingly 'perverse' results, such as a high level of social and economic deprivation sometimes being associated with a lower level of crime than that which emerges in a more affluent setting. These, after all, are the key features of actual data on crime.

Our model does in fact lead quite readily to results in which the proportion of criminals in the population can differ by a factor of ten or more, and in which apparently perverse behaviour exists. Figure 3.2, for example, plots the relationship between the level of social and economic deprivation and crime.

To obtain these results, we choose a set of values for the other factors in the model, such as the deterrence effect of the justice system, and keep these fixed. We then solve the model repeatedly for different values of the social and economic factors. This enables us to trace out how the proportion of criminals in the population varies with the level of deprivation.

We assume that, in terms of the flows between the different categories of the model, as the level of social and economic deprivation falls, the *qualitative* effect is always to reduce the proportion of criminals in the population. But the *quantitative* impact can vary enormously.

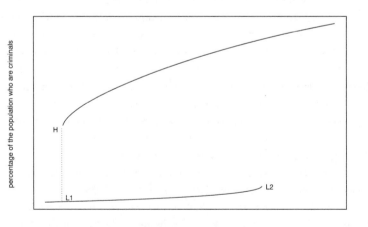

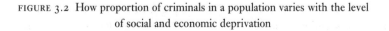

FIGURE 3.2 How proportion of criminals in a population varies with the level of social and economic deprivation

Suppose we start from a position on the higher of the two solid lines, at the very top right-hand corner of the chart. From here, reading down to the bottom axis tells us that there is a high level of deprivation. Reading across gives the proportion of criminals in the population, which is high.

Gradually, as we move down the line towards the left, reducing the level of deprivation, the proportion of criminals continues to fall. But, increasingly, for any given reduction in the level of deprivation, the impact on crime becomes stronger. At the critical level, where the solid line ends, marked by the letter 'H' (for 'high crime' levels), it tips the system to an entirely different position. This is indicated by the 'L1' point on the bottom solid line, connected to H by the dotted line. So, at the critical point 'H', even a very small further reduction in the level of deprivation leads to dramatically lower crime rates. Once we are on the bottom line, additional falls in deprivation reduce crime by only small amounts.

But suppose instead that we start at the bottom left-hand part of the chart, on the lower of the two solid lines, and observe the effects of increasing the levels of deprivation. In practice, this could happen even if a society were becoming more affluent at the overall level, for particular areas or groups in the population could miss out on the general prosperity – as indeed seems to be the case in America. Initially, increases in deprivation have little impact on crime, as we move along the curve past the point L1. Nothing dramatic starts to happen when we move in this direction, until we reach the point L2. Any further increase in deprivation leads to a large leap upwards on to the higher of the two solid lines, joining it directly above the L2 point.

This description of what happens to crime as the level of deprivation varies brings out the key features of the analysis, which in turn are reflected in the basic qualities of the real-world experience of crime rates.

First, even quite small changes in deprivation can lead to large changes in crime rates, as we see around the critical points H and L2. But, more generally, the relationship between changes in deprivation and changes in crime is not at all straightforward. The impact of any given change can vary dramatically depending upon the exact situation in which the change is made. Most of the time, a given small change in deprivation has only a small effect on crime; but sometimes this is rather more, and sometimes it is a very large one.

Importantly, the *same* level of deprivation can, depending on where we start from, be associated with substantially *different* rates of crime. For levels of deprivation between the points L1 and L2, we can either be on the bottom solid line, and experience low crime rates, or we can be on the top line, and suffer high ones.

This complexity is entirely typical of many economic and social situations. Thinking back to our basic ants model illustrated in Figure 1.1, we showed that knowing the proportion of the ant colony visiting one of the sites at any particular time gives us absolutely no information about what will happen to the proportions in the immediate future. From the same split of the colony between the two food sites, the proportions can move in either direction, by large or small amounts. In the crime model, there is more structure and content than this. We can *in principle* say useful things about what happens to crime rates when social and economic deprivation changes from any particular, existing level. But the relationship between the two is very complex and is not amenable to discovery by conventional analysis.

This complicated behaviour exists precisely because of the presence of social interaction, the factors which introduce the concept that the behaviour of individuals can be affected directly by the behaviour of others. In technical terms, the interactions introduce non-linearities which lead to the existence of multiple equilibrium points. But the process can be understood informally. Consider, for example, what happens when we examine the consequences of making the impact of social and economic deprivation gradually more important in the decision to become a criminal.

Not surprisingly, the model suggests that this leads to a gradual increase in the proportion of the population who are criminals. However, this in turn leads to feedbacks through the influence of the social interaction terms. As the proportion of criminals rises, this in itself makes it more likely that the proportion will increase still further. And the more of a population which is criminal, the weaker are the sanctions of social disapproval of the non-criminal part of the population, so the incentive to stop being a criminal is reduced.

Once a critical point is reached, the strength of these feedbacks intensifies, and the proportion of criminals rises rapidly and dramatically.

This does not mean that everyone eventually becomes a criminal, for the strengths of the various flows in the model will set limits to the proportion which ends up in this category. But it does mean that two populations, whose circumstances are very similar but who happen to lie either side of the critical point, will end up with dramatically different crime rates.

Another illustration is given by examining the effects of changes in the severity of the criminal justice system, given in Figure 3.3. We assume that the effect of, say, a more punitive criminal justice system is to reduce the proportion of criminals in the population. The harshness of the system is represented along the bottom of the graph, and the proportion of criminals in the population on the left-hand axis. Imagine that we start from a position in the top left-hand corner of Figure 3.3, where a very lax regime is associated with high levels of crime. What happens to crime when the justice system is made more punitive?

As the criminal justice system becomes more strict, it acts as a deterrent on crime and the proportion of criminals in the population falls. But the effect at first is rather minimal. Greater severity does reduce

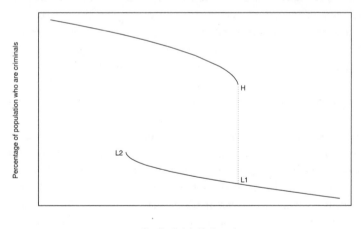

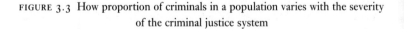

FIGURE 3.3 How proportion of criminals in a population varies with the severity of the criminal justice system

44

crime, but not by very much. This is shown by what happens as we move down the upper of the two solid lines. Gradually, as we move along the line to the right, for any given increase in the effectiveness of negative incentives, the impact on crime becomes stronger. At the critical level, where the solid line ends, marked by the letter 'H' to indicate 'high crime' levels, we once again experience a dramatic drop to the point L1 on the lower of the two solid lines.

This helps to illuminate the current debate on the desirability or otherwise of the 'zero-tolerance' policy of policing adopted with apparently great success in New York. The social interaction effects in the model imply that large and seemingly inexplicable changes in crime rates can take place. Inexplicable, that is, within the conventional mind-set which looks for simple cause and effect mechanisms. If the actual process which generates crime in New York were close to a critical level, the introduction of zero-tolerance could shift the system to a new, altogether lower level of crime. But this does not mean that the adoption of such a policy in other cities will necessarily have the same impact. A city which corresponds to the top left of our simplified model in Figure 3.3 would see only relatively minor changes in crime rates as a result of adopting the policy.

The features exhibited in Figures 3.2 and 3.3 are an important reason why the conventional literature on crime fails to arrive at a consensus about the impact of different policies on crime rates. With data taken from certain parts of Figure 3.3, say, the orthodox approach will work well, and show quite clearly that longer prison sentences, for instance, lead to lower crime. But, with other samples of data, the results will seem perverse. If a researcher were given data from a few points to the immediate left of point H on the top solid line combined with all the data to the left of this point on the bottom solid line, he or she would be forced to conclude that shorter sentences appeared to reduce crime, for that would be the information contained in that particular sample of data.

Our framework of analysis, stark though it may be in outline, has clear positive implications for policy. The complexities of the model are introduced by the terms which represent social interaction, the fundamental principle of the behaviour of our ants. It is the act of observing the behaviour of others and being induced to change one's own behaviour as a result which leads to these complexities. And this is such a basic and obvious feature of reality that it cannot be ignored by any approach which purports to offer insights into how crime develops.

CHAPTER 4

Family Values

The issue of changes in family structures is probably even more sensitive than that of crime. Major alterations in the structure of families in most Western countries have taken place in recent decades, which have led to acrimonious debates about the causes and consequences, overlaid as they are with views about the morality of different types of behaviour.

The key feature which any plausible theory must be able to explain is the reduction in the proportion of the adult population which is married, and the rise in the single (never married) and divorced proportions. To varying degrees, this has become common across the West since the 1960s.

Many simplistic, mono-causal arguments have been advanced to account for these shifts. The undermining of the traditional virtues of thrift and responsibility by the welfare state is one such point of view. But the complexity of the phenomenon cannot be dealt with so easily. This particular argument is hard to sustain because, for example, it is very hard to see any connection across countries between the *overall* extent of the welfare state and the degree to which the traditional family has declined. Some of the biggest changes have taken place in countries at both extremes of attachment to the welfare state, namely the United States and Sweden. Both weak and strong welfare states have coincided with massive changes in family structures. Such evidence does not necessarily mean that the hypothesis has no validity, but that other factors clearly have been equally or even more important.

Economists, as ever, regard economic factors as being responsible for shifts in family structures. And their models are considerably more sophisticated than most of the arguments which pass for serious debate in this area. As with crime, Gary Becker pioneered the introduction of rigorous, conventional economic analysis to the family in the late 1970s. Whatever criticisms may be made of applying economics to social questions such as crime and the family, it should be said that Becker's Nobel Prize was certainly deserved. His ideas were highly innovative and imaginative, and it is only by testing such concepts and thinking about their implications that we can ever make progress in our understanding of society.

According to the Becker model, the couple in a marriage are seen as a single economic unit which manages the division of labour between the home and paid employment in the formal sector of the economy so as to maximize the overall economic efficiency of the unit. This is a rather abstract way of thinking about the problem. But it does have the virtue of offering a realistic, if only partial, account of changes in family structures.

Suppose a husband and wife were identical in their level of education and training, their abilities, their attractiveness to employers, and in their tastes and preferences about working, staying at home, having children, and so on. It might be thought that it would not really matter how the couple divided their time between work and the home, for by assumption in this case both are equally good at whatever activity they choose.

But on Becker's logic, this is not so. The family unit would be better off if the man and wife nevertheless specialized, with one performing household tasks and the other getting a paid job outside the home. With each partner concentrating on one particular task, gains in efficiency can be made, or, in the jargon of economics, 'the gain comes from increasing returns to investments in sector-specific human capital that raise productivity'.

This is the essence of the economic theory of the family, though a further bit* must be added to give a complete account, on its own logic, as to why marriage exists. To illustrate this, imagine that everyone in a country were identical, just as our hypothetical couple introduced above. The gains from specialization could then apparently be made by one half of the population staying at home, and the other half going out to work,

---

* More exactly, two bits should be added. An explanation needs to be given as to why couples marry rather than cohabit. This issue has only been addressed by economic theory comparatively recently, and an excellent discussion is given by Bob Rowthorn – an economist not, in general, sympathetic to mainstream thinking – in the *Cambridge Journal of Economics*, 1999. It introduces issues such as contingent claims contracts which, although intellectually interesting, are not necessary to our main theme.

with everyone remaining single in their own separate homes. To avoid accusations of gender bias, we might imagine the allocation being made at random as to who worked and who stayed at home. Each worker could then pay a home specialist to look after his or her home. Everyone in this example has paid work, but some are paid for household work, and some are rewarded for work outside the home. By specializing, everything is made more efficient.

This may seem a bizarre example, but it seems to fit with the logic of the theory. Economics attempts to get round this by recognizing that many household tasks can be performed with greater overall efficiency if they are carried out on a larger scale. Many meals, for example, are not twice as difficult or costly to prepare for two people as they are for one. Further, services produced within the family unit can be more readily tailored to the specific tastes of the consumers – the members of the family – than can services bought outside, representing an additional area of gain.

The economic theory of the family, abstract though it is, does not stop there. The quality of children produced by the couple will, it is argued, be maximized if one of them focuses on bringing up children, gaining expertise over time and hence performing the task more efficiently. Becker contends that the most efficient division of labour ends up being along gender lines because women have, again in economics-speak, a 'comparative advantage' over men in the production and rearing of children.

We have now moved rapidly on to prickly ground. But Becker was most emphatically not trying to say how the world *ought* to be. Like a true scientist, he observed how the world actually is, and put forward a theory to try to explain it.

On this view, increases in women's employment and/or earnings will lead to a decline in marriage and a rise in divorce. In part, this is simply because independent living becomes more feasible. But increases in the earning opportunities of married women also reduce their gains from marriage. The more money a woman can earn in a job, the less the incentive, in general, to stay at home, and the less, in particular, the desire to have children becomes, for a large part of the cost of having children is the loss of earnings associated with this.

At the level of a broad overview, the theory appears to be consistent with what has happened to family structures in the West over the past thirty years or so. More and more women are working; for example, in the countries of the European Union the proportion of women at work has risen from 22 per cent in 1960 to some 45 per cent today. And their earnings have risen over time, even allowing for inflation. At the same time, married couples as a proportion of the adult population have fallen, and the proportions of singles and divorced have risen.

It is when the theory is examined in more detail that doubts begin to arise. In America, for example, highly educated women, who are in a stronger position in the labour market than less qualified ones, have higher rates of marriage than other groups. Indeed, just as with crime, an enormous academic literature exists on the validity of the pure economic approach to the evolution of family structures. And, as with crime, it is equally inconclusive. Some work supports the Becker thesis, and some appears to contradict it. But, regardless of the conclusion of any particular piece of work, it is hard to establish convincing connections between family changes and economic factors using conventional approaches.

The orthodox economic approach to the family purports to offer a general theory which accounts for phenomena such as changes in the rate of marriage and in fertility. It is able to give an explanation which is partially successful in some circumstances. But it does not account for the sheer diversity of experience of the Western countries in terms of family formation. While the general direction of trends in recent decades towards more single and divorced people and fewer marrieds is consistent across countries, at any point in time the structures differ substantially. In the mid-1990s, for example, the divorce rates in Denmark, Finland and the UK were some 25–50 per cent higher than in France and Germany, and more than double the rate in Italy.

Given that, overall, the economies of such countries are very similar, which is reflected in their income per head, the patterns are consistent with the hypothesis that non-economic, social factors also play a significant role in family formation. Attitudes towards marriage vary from country to country, and these presumably influence the different outcomes we see in countries which, in economic terms, are very similar.

Taking a much wider historical perspective than that of the West in the late twentieth century, changes in the rates of marriage and childbirth have been associated with quite different economic circumstances. For instance, after centuries of near-destitution, during the twelfth century Western Europe entered a period of comparative prosperity. Once the population had been fed, sufficient resources remained to build marvellous cathedrals, such as those at Paris, Canterbury and Chartres. In France alone, more than eighty new cathedrals were built at this time. According to orthodox economic theory, this increase in prosperity should have led to a decline in both marriage and fertility. But, on the contrary, the age at which people married fell sharply and there was a medieval baby boom.

David Hackett Fischer provides more evidence in his book *The Great Wave*. For example, the contemporary issue of single mothers is by no means a new phenomenon. There was a surge in births outside marriage in England in the late sixteenth and early seventeenth centuries, followed by a sharp fall. The eighteenth century saw this rate increase again, to be followed by a decline during the following century. All the time during this long period, England was becoming steadily more prosperous as she moved towards and into the Industrial Revolution. Yet the impact of increased prosperity clearly varied substantially over time.

All this points to the importance of attitudes and fashion, as it were, in changes in family structures. As in the world of our ants, the behaviour of an individual can be influenced directly by the behaviour of others. As we saw in the adaptation of the basic ants model to crime, this principle enables apparent paradoxes to be resolved, such as poverty being sometimes associated with low crime rates yet at other times being regarded as the cause of higher crime.

The logic of Becker's model is powerful, but in its pure economic form it is incomplete. High and low rates of marriage can be associated with, say, the same level of prosperity, and economic models need to be augmented with our ant behaviour in order to be compatible with this important fact.

As with the various categories in our crime model, the family structure of any population can be thought of as being made up of a set of stocks and flows. The stocks represent the numbers of individuals within each category or type of family in any given period, and the flows represent the changes in the stocks, such as the numbers who move from married to divorced, during that particular period.

The basic idea of our model is that at any point a person can be in one of a number of potential states – single, married or divorced. The aggregate flows between these states depend upon factors such as the severity or otherwise of the divorce laws, and the strength of economic incentives, including the level of female real incomes.

In addition, we introduce terms to capture the attitudinal process of social emulation, or social interaction. Specifically, the probability of any individual switching from single to married is related to the proportion of the population who are already married, and the probability of married individuals becoming divorced is also related to the proportion of the population who are divorced. So in this way, any given change in the overall economic incentive to marry could have quite different effects in two countries identical in every respect except for the initial pattern of family structure prevailing when the change is made.

There is a rich diversity of flows between different family structures, but the essential dynamics can be captured in a simple approach which examines just three categories of family structure: single and never married, married, and divorced. Again, the model can be made more complicated by introducing categories for, say, widows and cohabiting couples, but in the true scientific spirit, we start with a model – or map if we think of it this way – which is as straightforward as possible.

Schematically, the essence of the model can be set out very simply:

$$S \rightarrow M \rightleftarrows D$$

In other words, there is a flow from Single to Married, a flow from Married to Divorced and a flow back from Divorced into Married.

Consider in the first instance the flow from M to D. At the level of the individual, both the age one's parents married and their marital experience are known to be good predictors of the probability of divorce. But these proximate predictors are themselves dependent upon a complex mix of socio–economic and attitudinal factors.

The flow from M to D is assumed to depend in principle upon the net effect of economic factors and changes in the divorce laws. An important economic influence is the incentive for women to stay married rather than get divorced, embracing the issue of the economic independence of women, the availability of jobs, the level of pay, and any subsidies through the tax system to marriage. In addition, as already discussed above, the second key factor which determines the flow from M to D is that of social customs or attitudes.

Similarly, suppose the flow from S to M also depends upon two factors: first, the net effect of economic factors such as the general level of tax and benefit incentives, and the economic independence of women given by the level of real incomes and the rate of female labour participation. And, second, social customs.

We can examine the consequences of changing the values assigned to the various flows to see what their impact is. For example, Figure 4.1 shows what happens to the number of people who are married when the economic incentive to switch from being single to married varies, and when the incentive to stay married rather than get divorced also changes.

In this three-dimensional chart, the vertical axes show the number of people who are married. (The axis on the far left is labelled, although in principle the numbers could be read off from any of the vertical axes.) The axis on the right measures the economic incentive to move from the single to the married category, with incentives increasing towards the right of the diagram. The axis on the left plots the strength of the economic incentive to stay married rather than get divorced.

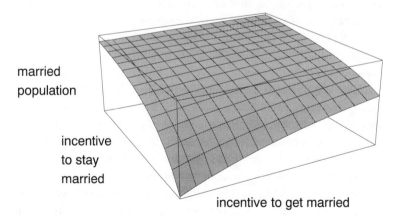

FIGURE 4.1 Impact of changes in economic incentives to marry and stay married

53

This chart can be read in a number of ways. At the very bottom of the plotted surface, where both the economic incentive effects are at their lowest values, we can read off the vertical axis that the number of people married is low. Holding the incentive to get married fixed at this low point, we can see what happens to the number of married people when the economic incentive to stay married is increased. We do this by moving diagonally along the axis labelled 'incentive to stay married', reading directly upwards on to the plotted surface, and then across to the vertical axis.

At first, the number of marrieds rises steeply even for relatively small changes in the incentive to stay married. But as the incentive is increased, the consequent increase in the stock of marrieds becomes smaller and smaller. Similarly, for any given level of incentives to stay married, the effect of changing the strength of the incentive to get married on the number of marriages is positive, but the impact of any given change becomes smaller, the stronger the effect already is.

The surface along which we move in the family model in Figure 4.1 is not as complex as for crime, but it is not completely straightforward. The impact of any given change can vary considerably, depending upon our starting point.

And there are further potential complications. For example, focusing our attention in the area near the very top part of the plotted surface, there appear to be limits on the number of people who can be persuaded to get married. The parts of the surface near the top right-hand corner show the number of marrieds when both economic incentives factors are strong. Yet it is clear that, in this area of the chart, increases in these factors lead to only small changes in the number of people who are married.

A simpler way of illustrating how different intensities of these flows would affect the outcome, and how the impacts vary depending upon the position from which we start, is given in Figure 4.2. This shows the effect on the number of marrieds of changing just one, rather than two, of the factors in the model, namely the economic incentive to stay married. Initially, small increases in economic incentives lead to large changes in the outcome, but the impact of further changes becomes less at higher levels of incentive.

Figure 4.2 is obtained by looking at Figure 4.1 from a different

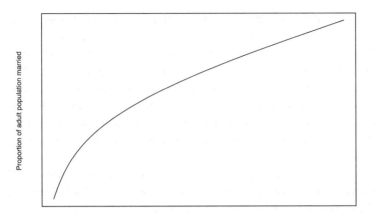

FIGURE 4.2 Impact of economic incentive to stay married: weak impact of social attitudes on behaviour

perspective. Instead of examining the whole surface, it is as if the box in Figure 4.1 were turned round so that we could only see one side of it – the side with axes which link changes in the economic incentive to stay married with the number of people who are married.

Figure 4.2 is labelled 'weak impact of social attitudes on behaviour'. But if we were to choose somewhat higher values of the impact of social attitudes, the relationships in the model become even more interesting. Figure 4.3 shows one such outcome.

As with the crime model, there are now two different levels of the proportion of the population which is married that are compatible, over a wide range, with the *same* level of economic incentive to stay married. There can be high and low solutions. Near the tipping points, small changes in the economic incentive can lead to large changes in marriage, both up and down. But elsewhere in the chart, for example along the solid line at the bottom left, quite large changes produce relatively little impact on marriage.

The complete picture of what happens to marriage when *both* the economic incentive to stay married and the impact of social attitudes on behaviour change is given by the rather exotic plot in Figure 4.4. Once

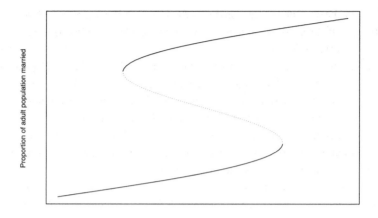

Economic incentive to stay married

FIGURE 4.3 Impact of economic incentive to stay married: strong impact of social attitudes on behaviour

again, the proportion of the population which is married is plotted on the vertical axis. On the axis moving diagonally to the right from the very bottom corner is the strength of the economic incentive to stay married.

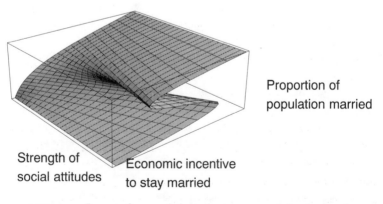

FIGURE 4.4 Impact of economic incentive to stay married and strength of social attitudes.

And on the axis moving diagonally to the left from the same place is the strength of the social attitude terms, the effect of the behaviour of others on any given individual.

Some parts of the plotted surface look very similar to that of Figure 4.1, like a mattress which sags in parts but is more or less in shape. These parts of the chart correspond to situations in which relationships between marriage and any single factor in the model are reasonably well-behaved, as for example in Figure 4.2. Here, the connection between marriage and the economic incentive to stay married is not completely straightforward, but it is not subject to leaps and discontinuities.

But other parts of Figure 4.4 look like a mattress which is not merely sagging but has been rather violently folded over on itself. It is in these areas of the chart where the really interesting effects take place, where small changes of any particular influence on marriage can lead to substantial shifts in the outcome. And it is in such parts that conventional analysis finds it very difficult to come up with meaningful results. Sometimes, small changes will lead to small ones, and, in situations not too far away, the same change will result in a major shift.

Reality, of course, is far more complex even than the world of our simplified model. But a failure to recognize its complexity, and persisting in the mind-set in which policy-makers have been schooled, means that serious errors can arise. Sometimes, in some the parts of the system, this approach may lead to success. But in less well-behaved areas, the wrong conclusions can easily be drawn. Once again, the impact of the behaviour of others on any individual needs to be an essential ingredient of any approach that has the potential to offer satisfactory accounts of a complex phenomenon.

Voting behaviour, crime and the structure of families are all social themes to which variants of the principles which account for the behaviour of our ants can be applied. And, as we saw in Chapter 2, so are diverse economic phenomena such as what determines a blockbuster or a flop in the film industry, why financial markets are inherently highly volatile, why inferior products sometimes drive superior competitors out of business, and why some regions suddenly prosper while neighbouring ones can languish in depression.

It is not that orthodox economics offers no account of such things. It does. But its explanations are at best only partial and at worst potentially misleading. Perhaps it is time to step aside to see what has gone on in the world of conventional economic theory.

CHAPTER 5

'Use the Maths, then Burn It'

The scholars who established the basis for modern economics in the late Victorian era knew perfectly well that the tastes and behaviour of individuals are not fixed, but are often directly influenced by how others behave. This kind of conduct has existed since time immemorial. In the sumptuous court of Louis XIV of France, for example, the consumption of fresh peas became a fetish, so that gentlemen and ladies who had dined on some of the best food in Europe would hurry home to gobble peas and boast the next day of the number they had consumed before bedtime.

Nearer to our own times, at the turn of the century the American Thorsten Veblen documented a whole mode of conspicuous consumption in his book *The Theory of the Leisure Class*. The more an object is acquired by others, the more the behaviour of any individual is likely to be altered so that he or she now desires the same thing, whereas previously the thought of owning the object had never been entertained.

But when, at the same time as Veblen was writing, economists were developing their theories to try to describe how the world operates, they were obliged to make the simplifying assumption that the tastes and preferences of individuals in their models *were* fixed. This was not because of stupidity – far from it – but because the mathematical tools required to analyse such processes did not then exist. As we saw in the opening chapter, the fundamental properties of the world of our ants, which has so many parallels in human behaviour, can only be understood properly using both the power of computers and mathematical results which were only obtained in the 1980s.

A hundred years ago, the ability to analyse the consequences of ant behaviour, in which an individual can be influenced directly by the behaviour of others, lay beyond the frontiers of scientific knowledge. But an illustration of the care which earlier economists took in thinking about the world can be seen in the work of Alfred Marshall, who occupied a chair in economics at Cambridge and who was regarded as the leading economist in the world in the decades around the turn of the century.

Marshall led a very modest and cloistered existence. He entered St John's College, Cambridge, as an undergraduate in 1862 and, apart from a few years around 1880, he spent the rest of his long life in that institution. He wrote occasional letters to the national press, but his role in public affairs was minimal.

Compared to the 1990s, when it seems that almost any charlatan with a smattering of knowledge is only too eager to pontificate about the economy on behalf of some financial institution or other, Marshall's detachment is remarkable. He wrote to a colleague, 'My only confident dogma in economics is that every short statement on a broad issue is inherently false. It was in 1903 that the Chancellor of the Exchequer set me two questions . . . it is now 1909 and the answers are not yet ready.' With characteristic politeness, however, and without any apparent irony, Marshall did send an immediate short reply to the hapless Chancellor, saying, 'I am telling my servant to send you a copy of a paper I wrote in 1890.'

For all his seeming unworldliness, Marshall in his writings was constantly concerned with the need to illustrate principles with examples from real life. His views on the use of mathematics in economics are worth quoting, not least because Marshall himself had extensive training in the subject, graduating in second place amongst the maths students of his year at Cambridge. Again in correspondence, he wrote, 'I have had a growing feeling that a mathematical theorem dealing with economic hypotheses is very unlikely to be good economics, and I go more and more on the rules – 1) Use mathematics as a shorthand language rather than as an engine of inquiry. 2) Keep to them until you have done. 3) Translate into English. 4) Then illustrate by examples that are important in real life. 5) Burn the mathematics. 6) If you can't succeed in 4, burn 3. This last I do often.'

In many ways, the approach adopted in this book deliberately tries to follow these invaluable rules which Marshall laid down. Although the analysis is underpinned by the maths of non-linear probability, whether it is ants, the foreign exchange markets or Hollywood, crime or the family, we are attempting to understand in English both what is going on in the technical bits of the work, and how this fits in with what actually happens.

Marshall's main work, the *Principles of Economics*, is full of insights into a wide range of problems. Most of his efforts in the last thirty years or so of his life were concentrated upon refining and extending his *magnum opus*. But its importance in the economics profession for many years was that it represented the most comprehensive articulation so far of the theory of how best to allocate a given amount of resources. This, indeed, was its main purpose and the reason why Marshall was regarded so highly by his contemporaries.

Individuals in this theory do not operate in *complete* isolation from each other. But the existence of other individuals is acknowledged only in a very restrictive sense. A classic way of illustrating the economics of supply and demand, the essence of conventional theory, is the market stall. An individual may, for example, relish bananas and go out to buy some from this hypothetical stall. The consequences of decisions made by everyone else in the neighbourhood about how many bananas to purchase will affect the price. If the demand for bananas is high relative to the available supply, the seller will put the price up. It is this *indirect* consequence of the behaviour of others which is allowed to affect the behaviour of our hypothetical banana-loving individual. The higher the price, the less he or she will buy.

The theory permits the behaviour of others to influence the behaviour of any given individual through the effect of their decisions on price. It does not allow individual behaviour to be influenced directly by others, so the number of bananas bought at a *given* price would not be affected by how many other people buy. In the context of the banana market, such a proposition may seem absurd. But in the world of fashion and consumer crazes, stranger things have happened. In the children's toy market, or in the music industry, as the number of people who own a particular item increases, the behaviour of others is altered so that they, too, desire the same item. Whatever might be the intrinsic attractions of Ninja Turtles, Cabbage Patch dolls or Buzz Lightyear, the fact that many children either already owned or longed to own them meant that each, in their time, became the *ne plus ultra* of every child's Christmas stocking.

Of course, this does not apply to all items of consumption, and we often observe reactions against fashion. No self-respecting member of the British middle class, for example, would be seen dead on the Spanish Mediterranean coast once this had become a favoured holiday destination for the criminals and working class amongst their fellow countrymen. But even here, the same principle of altered behaviour is at work, except this time in the reverse direction: the more certain kinds of people want a product, the less another group do.

Contemporary economists can hardly be unaware of this effect. Their television screens are bombarded on a twenty-four-hour basis by advertising, a massive industry dedicated solely to the proposition that tastes and behaviour *can* be changed directly. A fortune in consultancy fees awaits the lucky economist who can demonstrate that the huge sums spent by the world's largest companies on advertising are a complete waste of money, but so far there are no successful claimants.

But in general, economists are still perfectly happy to work with the assumption that the tastes and preferences of individuals are fixed. Why should this be? There are three main reasons why the type of behaviour exemplified by our ants is ignored in standard economic theory. The first is, in the main, excusable. It was not really possible for Marshall to investigate in a rigorous way the implications of allowing the behaviour of individuals to affect those of others directly. The relevant tools did not exist until the 1980s.* But it is no longer the case. So the second reason why economists ignore this behaviour does little credit to the profession. Particularly in the past twenty years or so, many economists have become carried away with the technical virtuosities of their standard theories. And it seems that they have forgotten the highly restrictive assumptions which have to be made for the model to have any degree of validity. Relaxing these assumptions so as to offer a more realistic view of how people actually behave, is threatening to many economists. Any model is a drastic simplification of reality. But relaxing the assumption that the tastes and behaviour of every individual are fixed leads to results which are very different from those of the orthodox model of economics. The theorems which they have struggled so hard as graduate students to master, and the policy prescriptions which they now so freely offer, are no longer relevant in many situations.

The third reason, it must be acknowledged, is that conventional

---

* Robin Marris's *Managerial Capitalism*, published in 1964, contains the most sophisticated earlier attempt to formalize the concept of interacting agents in the context of consumer demand theory. But this is just one of a number of strikingly original insights in that book.

economic theory does give a partially successful view of how the world operates. Thinking back to the foreign exchange and stock markets discussed in Chapter 2, orthodox theory implies that changes in the prices of assets in these markets are inherently unpredictable. And an enormous amount of empirical testing suggests that this is true. The problem for conventional theory is how to account for the high degree of volatility which is observed. Once we allow the principles of behaviour of our ants into the model, and permit traders to be influenced directly by the behaviour of others, we have a theory which explains more things than does the orthodox approach: it, too, suggests that asset prices cannot be predicted, but it also explains why such a high degree of volatility exists.

In some circumstances, conventional economics finds it very hard to give a plausible account of what actually happens. The choice between competing brands of video recorders, where an inferior product succeeded in driving its superior rival out of business, is one such example.

However, there is a range of situations in which orthodoxy tells a relatively satisfactory story about the real world. Some examples will be given shortly, which tend to be characterized by the fact that individuals have to process only a very limited amount of information. Much of the direct interaction between agents that influences preferences has already taken place before individuals find themselves in these particular situations.

The central core of economic theory from the 1870s onwards has been concerned with how a given amount of resources can be allocated most efficiently amongst individual consumers and companies. It has come to be known as the theory of competitive, or general, equilibrium, and its theorems pervade a great deal of policy discussion in the West.

The theory is based on a series of postulates about human behaviour and the workings of the economy. Designed as a logical description of how rational individuals and companies ought to behave, the emphasis lies equally on the words 'rational' and 'individual'. Individuals act so as to maximize the value of their own circumstances. Firms, for example, are interested in profits, so are deemed to act in a way which maximizes profits. Individuals are concerned with their 'utility' – the jargon term for their overall well-being – and hence are assumed to behave so that their utility is maximized. But the tastes and preferences of every individual agent, whether a person or a company, are assumed to be fixed. Ants have no place in this particular world.

In limited contexts, the theory can provide a reasonable approximation to reality. If prices rise in a specific market, for example, demand usually falls, either because some people stop buying altogether or because everyone cuts back consumption a bit. And if supply is curtailed for whatever reason, the price will be observed to rise.

One of the most delightful illustrations of this latter assumption was provided in a memorable sequence from the old television programme, *The Untouchables*. Elliot Ness and his men have had a success in restricting the availability of cocaine in Chicago. Frank Nitti, the enforcer for gangster Al Capone, in a terrifying rage, demonstrates his ignorance of the basic precepts of free-market economics: 'The price of cocaine in this city is sky-high,' he froths to his trembling subordinates, 'and you punks can't even get me a single ounce to sell!'

There is, of course, a multitude of examples from real life of the workings of the price mechanism and the interaction of supply and demand in specific contexts. For instance, shortly after the Russian Revolution, a grandiose policy known as War Communism was introduced, in which every aspect of the economy was to be planned and regulated. Orlando Figes in his monumental work *A People's Tragedy* describes one such measure. All the production of grain and vegetables throughout Russia was subjected to a levy, with the state seizing a large part of the produce according to fixed quotas. But, by bureaucratic oversight, onions were omitted from the list. A massive boom in onion production soon followed, this being the one vegetable that could be sold at a profit.

In our own day, in a rather more subtle example, several higher education institutes in Britain were upgraded to the status of universities in the 1990s. One of these, Thames Valley University, attracted a great deal of unfavourable publicity when it became known that students who had failed their exams were being allowed to proceed as though they had passed. The consensus in the educational world was that this action had substantially damaged the university. However, the next year saw a record number of student applications to Thames Valley – by far the biggest increase in the whole British university sector. Clearly, students who were weaker academically, but not lacking in worldly wisdom, reasoned that it was easier to get a degree there than anywhere else. In other words, the price of getting a degree, measured in terms of effort and ability, was presumed to have fallen, and in consequence the demand for places rose.

The large amount of accurate information available from electronic point of sale machines in supermarkets allows rigorous testing of certain precepts in the orthodox theory of consumer behaviour, although very few academic economists seem to have appreciated its existence. Data is readily accessible for, say, the sales of various brands of baked beans or whisky at specific prices in a particular store or chain of stores. Statistical techniques can be used to measure the impact on the sales of different brands as prices change over time. The basic principles of the theory, if not its more abstruse requirements, are almost invariably confirmed. But in this context, the potential purchaser, confronted by the different brands on the shelves, has already taken many relevant decisions. He or she has already decided to buy whisky, and to purchase it in that particular store rather than elsewhere. In short, most of the important decisions have already been taken, and a strictly limited amount of information, namely that of the prices of the brands, has to be processed.

We can think of the interactions of our ant world as having already taken place. An individual's decision to buy whisky rather than, say, beer, can obviously be influenced by the diktats of fashion. And within the whisky market, some brands will acquire more status than others by exactly the same process. When the individual arrives at the supermarket, all these influences have already been at work. The choice of which brand to buy has been restricted to the small number of alternatives which the individual deems acceptable. All that remains is to compare their relative prices, process this according to his or her already-shaped preferences, and pick the appropriate one.

Some may object that even this limited amount of information processing is far too difficult a task for many. The Basic Skills Agency carried out a survey of 6,000 men and women in seven developed economies. Without access to a calculator, they were asked to solve twelve elementary problems in arithmetic, such as 'subtract 1.78 from 5' and 'multiply 6 by 21'. Those in Japan scored highest, but even then only 43 per cent of all Japanese got all the questions right. In Britain, only 20 per cent succeeded in giving correct answers to them all. A rather more esoteric finding by *Newsweek* also casts doubt on the general ability to process information rationally: almost one-third of American citizens believe that the US government is in regular contact with aliens.

The standard response of economists is that it is 'as if' consumers are able to carry out more sophisticated calculations when basing decisions on the various prices which confront them. Provided it is not pushed too far, this argument does have a degree of plausibility. After all, very few cricketers or baseball players are capable of solving with pencil and paper the non-linear differential equations which govern the flight of the ball. Yet, with the exception of the English cricket team, they still manage to catch it.

As a description of how individuals behave in choosing amongst competing brands in a supermarket, the conventional theory of behaviour performs reasonably well. But the point cannot be emphasized too strongly that the amount of information that needs to be processed is restricted to a small number of prices of different brands.

In many decisions, the potential amount of information involved and the degree of sophistication required to analyse it are greater by several orders of magnitude. How individual agents, whether people or firms, respond in such circumstances is an important point to which we return later in this chapter.

But first of all, we need to think about the consequences of processing information for decisions that may have important implications for the future. Within reason, the amount of baked beans, or even of whisky, bought by someone on a trip to the local store is unlikely to be of any great consequence for their actions and circumstances in the future. In contrast, decisions about taking out a loan, buying a house, or whether or not to commit a crime, may well be of serious import for many years to come.

Individuals' ability, or rather lack of it, to process information efficiently about future consequences creates a very serious internal problem for the theory of competitive equilibrium.

In many ways, the most devastating criticisms of conventional theory have come from highly accomplished mathematical economists working entirely within the orthodox framework. In their efforts to refine the core model, to formulate it in a more rigorous way, they have made clear the gulf which separates developed market economies from the world of economic theory. Above all, they have shown that the key theorems of competitive equilibrium hold only in a timeless world. When the unknown future is introduced into the model, its basic results no longer obtain. Orthodox economic theory has two fundamental propositions. First, that the price mechanism operates to ensure that demand will equal supply in every single market. Imbalances cannot persist, but will be smoothed away by the negative feedback generated by the price mechanism. Second, in such an equilibrium, no individual or company can be made better off by altering the allocation of resources without making at least one person or company worse off. In other words, the distribution of income and wealth which emerges in the equilibrium cannot be altered by policies of taxation without making someone else worse off.

These results follow logically from the assumptions on which the theory is based. They are by no means intuitively obvious, and their establishment represents a formidable intellectual construct. Amongst other things, they have strong implications for the role of government, or rather the lack of it. In this ideal world, all markets clear by definition, so the authorities do not need to intervene to balance supply and demand. Further, any attempts to alter the allocation of resources will make at least one person worse off. In short, either economic policy has no effects, or it harms some group of citizens. Therefore there is no role for it.

Unfortunately for the theory, in 1982 David Newbery of Cambridge and Joseph Stiglitz of Princeton proved that in an uncertain world in which the future is allowed to exist, the conclusion that the distribution of income and wealth cannot be altered without harming someone is, in general, not true. Despite this finding, the old result continues to be taught to students the world over.

The exclusion of time from the theoretical model of competitive equilibrium began to attract serious attention from economists in the immediate post-war years. After all, uncertainty about the future is such a pervasive and obvious property of everyday life. The American Nobel prizewinner Kenneth Arrow made an important contribution to the problem in the early 1950s. He was able to prove the existence of competitive equilibrium – in other words to demonstrate that the price mechanism would ensure that demand always equalled supply – in a world in which the uncertain future existed. But, as Arrow himself realized perfectly well, he could only do this by incorporating uncertainty in a very restrictive way. In the standard, timeless version of the theory, a set of prices has to be discovered which ensures that supply and demand are equal in all markets. But actions which are taken today may very well have consequences in the future. So, at any point in time, once the future is allowed to exist, a set of prices must be found which will clear all markets not just today, but tomorrow, the day after tomorrow and so on, until, literally, the end of time.

Arrow was able to show that such prices could always be found, but only under extremely restrictive assumptions. Each individual in his model has to prepare a complete list of all future states of the world which might exist, and everyone must hold identical beliefs regarding the prices which would prevail in every conceivable state of the world in the future. Moreover, these views on prices have to be completely correct. In other words, everyone knows for certain what all prices will be in any particular state of the world at any time in the future. Individuals are permitted to be uncertain only in the very specific sense that they do not know what state of the world will actually obtain.

A simple example of this is a farmer producing wheat. The price of wheat at each point in the future will depend to a large extent on the weather and hence the state of the harvest. In Arrow's model, the farmer is assumed to know what the price of wheat will be at any time in the future regardless of the weather and the state of the harvest. In other words, he knows the exact price of wheat which will obtain for every conceivable combination of weather and harvest. And all other farmers hold identical views. What he and they do not know is what the weather will actually be.

Arrow's results were a major breakthrough. For the first time since its inception almost a century previously, the future had been incorporated into the model of competitive equilibrium. But, transparently, the world in Arrow's model bears no resemblance to reality, and some of the best minds in economics worked on the problem of how to introduce the uncertain future into the model in a more realistic way.

The definitive result was established by the American mathematical economist Roy Radner in an outstanding paper published in 1968. Working within the confines of the model of competitive equilibrium, he was able to relax Arrow's assumptions dramatically. He proved that a set of prices always existed which would clear all markets now and in the future, even if different people had different beliefs about the future state of the world. But there was a cost. For Radner's proof to be valid, everyone had to have access to a literally infinite amount of computational capacity.

This was the logical conclusion of a theory which postulates that individuals act in a way which maximizes their well-being, whether this takes the form of profits or the less tangible concept of utility. Even if all the other assumptions made by the theoretical model of competitive equilibrium are retained, Radner's conclusion is that the model 'breaks down completely in the face of limits on the ability of agents to compute optimal strategies'. In other words, even though the principle of acting so as to maximize profits seems a very plausible strategy for companies to follow, in an uncertain world firms are simply not able to decide the course of action which will unequivocally maximize profits.

This result has profound implications for how we might best describe the behaviour of individuals. The hypothesis that individuals act as maximizers seems perfectly logical and reasonable taken at face value. After all, it would seem to require a saint-like devotion to the welfare of others not to want to maximize one's own interests. Such minority categories aside, the concept that maximizing is the basis for individual behaviour seems entirely rational.

It is only when the implications are thoroughly explored, as in Radner's paper, that insoluble problems arise. The game of chess provides a simple illustration of the impossibility of following a maximizing strategy in practice. An immense amount of intellectual effort has been devoted to the game, and there is an enormous number of books and articles written by highly talented players giving advice as to what to do in a variety of situations. But a very simple question remains unanswered. At the start of the game, it is White to move. What is the best move White can make? No one knows. Some moves appear to be better than others, and much of the literature is devoted to examining just two of the twenty legal moves available to White at the start of the game. But it is impossible to work out all the possible permutations of a game, for these are so many as to defy the imagination – vastly exceeding, for example, the number of atoms in the entire universe. So it is impossible to know White's best move at the start of the game, the one that maximizes the chance of winning.

Even after the first move, most practical situations in chess offer so many possible permutations of continuations that it remains impossible to discover the best move, even with access to the world's fastest computers to perform the calculations. Instead of trying to work out the best move, players choose instead to make moves that look to offer them good prospects. Strong players make better moves than weak ones, but even Deep Blue, the computer that beat the world champion, cannot discover the unequivocally best move to make, except in highly simplified positions.

Managing a company such as General Motors, Microsoft or Shell Petroleum is at least as hard as playing a game of chess. But in the same way that in most circumstances the best move in chess can never be identified, it is rarely possible to say what is the optimal strategy for a company to follow. The boards of these companies include highly skilled and experienced business people, with access to enormous amounts of information and analysis. They undoubtedly try to come up with good strategies for their firms. And as in chess, good company boards come up with good strategies more often than bad ones. But the hypothesis of maximization requires that they consistently come up with not merely good plans, but optimal ones – the best that could possibly be chosen. Given the complexity of the problems which face them, the wisdom of Solomon would be unlikely to guarantee such an outcome.

Even in the special and very limited circumstances in which an unequivocal best choice does exist, in the words of psychologist David Good of Cambridge, 'Humans are bad at conforming to the exacting standards of models of sound reason.' Good cites the example of the so-called Monty Hall problem, which tends to lead otherwise sane and rational citizens to the heights of frenzied argument. A game-show contestant, having undergone the standard ritual humiliation involved in such contests, has won the right to choose to open one of three doors, A, B or C. Behind two doors lies a plastic duck to float in the bath, and behind the other is $10,000. The contestant wins whatever is behind the door of his or her choice. Amidst the mounting excitement of the audience, door A is chosen. Monty, the host, heightens the tension by opening door C (Monty knows what is behind each door), to reveal a duck. The contestant is given the chance to alter the decision, to choose B rather than A. What is to be done? Readers might like to cover up the next paragraph and work out – not guess – the answer.

In practice, most people refuse to change their decision. But switching to door B is always the best strategy to follow, for the simple fact that it doubles the chance of winning the $10,000. There is a 1 in 3 chance of the money being behind door A, and a 2 in 3 chance of it being behind B and C together. If you know there is zero chance of it being behind C – because Monty has opened it up for you – then there is a 2 in 3 chance of it being behind B. As David Good notes, 'Many people find it hard to understand the reasoning even when it is explained.'

From the perspective of the mathematics of probability theory, this is a very simple problem, in which all the relevant information is available and an unequivocal answer exists, yet people usually get it wrong. In more complex circumstances, the scope for misunderstanding and wrong decisions is enhanced enormously, even in the most elevated intellectual circles. The Cambridge Economics Faculty hosts the Marshall lectures, an extremely prestigious short lecture series which scholars from around the world are invited to give. Some years ago, when the faculty was still in the hands of the old Left, after bitter and prolonged fraternal dispute, it was agreed that Ernest Mandel, a Belgian Trotskyist, should be invited. The responsibility for issuing the invitation belonged to the chair of the faculty, a very distinguished elderly gentleman who was somewhat hard of hearing. Weeks passed, and nothing was announced. Mutterings of dark conspiracies grew, which were apparently confirmed when posters appeared announcing the lectures – to be given by Robert Mundell, a distinguished free-market American economist. Great was the consternation, but nothing sinister had happened. The faculty chair had simply never heard of Mandel, and had assumed all along that his colleagues must have been referring to Mundell.

Disquiet over the hypothesis that individuals are able to behave as maximizers has existed within economics for many years. Keynes, for example, was deeply sceptical about the concept, arguing in the 1930s that 'our existing knowledge does not provide a sufficient basis for a calculated mathematical expression [of forecasts]'. In essence, he suggested that individuals and companies were incapable of distilling the information available to them and turning it into a neat, mathematical formula which would give an optimal prediction of the future. In the early 1950s, at the same time that Arrow was extending orthodox theory to encompass the future, the French economist and subsequent Nobel prizewinner Maurice Allais was drawing attention to systematic patterns of behaviour which run directly counter to the maximization hypothesis.*

In more recent years, research programmes have been carried out which use the experimental techniques of behavioural psychology to try to test the validity of the view that individuals behave as if they were rational maximizers. For example, experiments are run in which it is possible to compute the optimal strategy to follow in a particular set of circumstances. In other words, there is a very limited amount of information to be processed, and there is a best way for an individual to behave. Real people are given real rewards if they succeed in discovering this course of action. The British economist Graham Loomes, together with various colleagues, has been prominent in this work over a number of years. His results and other, related research have challenged the orthodox theory of individual behaviour, which has led to a number of attempts to refine the theory to try to deal with the empirical problems that have been revealed. But in his latest paper, published in the prestigious *Economic Journal* in early 1998, Loomes concludes that the postulates of conventional theory are fundamentally flawed. The quest, he writes, to model individuals as if they are characterized by some set of fully formed and highly articulated preferences, which they can and will apply consistently to any and every form of decision problem, is doomed. Not just difficult: doomed.

Maximizing behaviour, for all its faults, is a valuable security blanket for many economists. It enables the mathematics of differential calculus to be applied to their theories, and for some intellectually satisfying results to be obtained. It has the side-benefit, too, of inducing mortal terror in

---

* The lack of immediate impact of his important article on this topic may be due to the fact that he was both writing in French *and* attacking Americans at the height of the Cold War. Allais's article is entitled 'Le comportement de l'homme rational devant le risque: critique des postulates et axiomes de l'école Americaine'.

many scholars from other disciplines in the social sciences who lack the required amount of mathematical training.

And, once the concept is abandoned, how are we to decide which of the myriad alternative modes of behaviour to include in our theories? The maximizing model has a pedigree of over a hundred years during which it has been polished and refined. In the new, uncharted areas there are many places marked, as on ancient maps, through lack of knowledge, 'Here be dragons.'

The hypotheses about behaviour which are made in a particular context should be thought of as guides, as rules of thumb, not to optimal, but to reasonably good behaviour. This argument has been advanced forcefully for many years by the American Herbert Simon, who was awarded the Nobel prize in economics. Simon describes the basic motivation underlying many forms of behaviour as 'satisficing' – not in the sense of wanting to maximize satisfaction, à la Mick Jagger, but of trying to develop and follow guidelines which are likely to lead to satisfactory outcomes.

This idea characterizes the world inhabited by our ants and the various applications of its principles of behaviour which rapidly lead to situations of great complexity. Indeed, it is only by using the analytical techniques of the ants model, and appropriate variations thereof, that the insights of Simon can be both formalized and put into practice.

Predicting how the system as a whole will behave is, as we have seen, either extremely difficult or literally impossible. It is not feasible in these circumstances to compute the 'best' strategy to follow, for the behaviour of the system itself is unpredictable: even if we knew for certain the laws of behaviour which the individual ants followed, we could never use these to predict where the system will be at any point in time.

The ants manage to take sensible decisions when confronted by an enormously complex system. An ant emerges from the nest to go out to find food. An excellent, indeed a possibly maximizing, strategy would be to get into a helicopter, scan the ground over a radius of several miles using American spy-plane equipment, and land on the best food site. But this option is not open to the ant. Instead, it follows some simple rules which have a good chance of working. If an individual has found food before at a particular site, a reasonable thing to do is to go back to the same place. Occasionally, it might pay to change direction and try somewhere else, for there may be an even more satisfactory food pile in the vicinity of the nest. And, finally, the ant might pay attention to the trails being left by returning ants who have found food. If they have found food at a different site, it might be worth a visit, because the food at the previously visited site might have run out; lacking a helicopter, the ant has no way of knowing in advance.

It seems fairly safe to assume that foreign-exchange dealers are human and hence are more intelligent than ants. We may occasionally have our doubts, but broadly speaking this is true. Yet, as we saw in Chapter 2, following the same principles of behaviour as the ants seems to be a reasonable way to behave in this more complicated context.

The rules of thumb which agents – people, firms – follow will be specific to the structure of the decision to be made. In other words, each problem needs to be addressed in its own way. While similarities may exist between different sets of circumstances, we will never find *the* rules of behaviour which agents follow in *all* circumstances. For they do not exist.

These behavioural principles of models in economics and the more general social sciences should conform to the basic scientific rule of being firmly rooted in empirical evidence. The evidence could be from a discipline such as psychology or criminology, supporting the postulates made in a specific application. Or it could show that the behavioural hypotheses lead to outcomes which are similar to those we actually observe.

The empirical mode of thought lies at the very heart of the success of the West. It underlay the discussion in the opening chapters when we examined a wide range of phenomena, from success and failure in the film industry, to the foreign exchange markets, and the ebbs and flows in crime rates. In order to try to understand what happens in each of these diverse examples, we put forward simple rules of thumb for the behaviour of individuals. The precise nature of the rules varies according to the problem being analysed, but they can all be related to the basic principle of our ants: the behaviour of an individual can be influenced directly by the behaviour of others. This apparently simple rule allows us to arrive at a much better understanding of complex phenomena.

CHAPTER 6

The Illusion of Control

The deep human desire to try to predict and control, and hence improve, our lot was expressed at an elevated level by T. S. Eliot in 'The Dry Salvages':

> To communicate with Mars, converse with spirits,
> To report the behaviour of the sea monster,
> Describe the horoscope, haruspicate or scry,
> Observe disease in signatures, evoke
> Biography from the wrinkles of the palm
> And tragedy from fingers; release omens
> By sortilege, or tea leaves . . .
>   . . . all these are usual
> Pastimes and drugs, and features of the press:
> And always will be . . .

On a more mundane note, in the process of thinking about this chapter, a splendid headline in the press caught my eye: 'Tarot card callers warned of unforeseen phone bills'. Something called the Association of Telephone Tarot and Associated Psychic Services had drawn attention to the various tricks which were being played on those who phoned, at premium rates, to have their fortunes read. One unfortunate gullible was kept on the line for over two hours when the person reading his fortune said he was going into a trance and should not be woken. In a similar vein, a few years ago the editor of a popular British newspaper began his letter of dismissal to the paper's astrology correspondent with the phrase 'As you will already know. . .'

Illusions about prediction are widespread. Indeed, a great deal of economic policy-making in the West is based upon delusions that short-term prediction and control of the economy are feasible. This topic forms the substance of this chapter.

Governments of all ideological persuasions spend a great deal of time worrying about how the economy will develop in the short term, over the next couple of years. If the anxiety levels of politicians were the only issue, few would be concerned. But our representatives do not merely contemplate the short-term future, they seek to influence it. Elaborate forecasts are prepared, not just by governments but by academic institutions and commercial companies. Advice is freely offered as to how the prospects for the economy can be improved, by an alteration to income-tax rates here, or a touch of public expenditure there. But the control which governments believe they have – in their ability to make reasonably accurate forecasts and to understand the consequences of policy changes designed to alter the outcome – is largely illusory.

As we have seen, in the world of our ants consistently accurate short-term predictability is inherently impossible. Given that many economists persist in seeing the world as a machine, a different analogy may help to illuminate the theme. Real scientists can actually land a spacecraft on the moon, because they have a very good knowledge of where the rocket is going and of what will happen if they adjust the controls. But economics lacks this understanding. Forecasters have a pretty good grasp of where the rocket is at any point in time,* but have little idea of the direction in which it is heading. Further, if they shift the controls, some of them say it will move the spaceship to the left, and others say it will move to the right. In such circumstances, it would be absolutely amazing if a successful moon landing were achieved. Yet this is exactly the situation in which conventional economic modellers find themselves and, truly remarkably, politicians continue to believe them.

The idea that short-term fluctuations in the overall economy, the booms and recessions of what is called the 'business cycle', are intrinsically unpredictable is not new in economics. Milton Friedman argued in the early 1950s that short-term government intervention was just as likely to accentuate the fluctuations of the business cycle as it was to dampen them. In essence, he was very sceptical that governments

---

* Strictly speaking, this may not always be true. Unlike data in the natural sciences, a great deal of economic data is subject to revision over time as more information comes to light. So forecasters may sometimes not even know exactly where the rocket has been in the recent past.

could anticipate events with sufficient accuracy. By luck, some individual governments would get the timing of their interventions right and succeed in containing the strength of booms and slumps, but their unlucky counterparts would only succeed in intensifying the fluctuations in their economies.

Even before Friedman wrote, there had been many distinguished examples of forecasting failure. J. K. Galbraith, in his book *The Great Crash 1929*, tells the story of the Harvard Economic Society: 'an extra curricular enterprise conducted by a number of economics professors of unexceptional conservatism. The purpose of the Society was to help businessmen foretell the future. Forecasts were made several times a month and undoubtedly gained in stature from their association with the august name of the university.' Galbraith relates that in early 1929 the Society decided that a mild recession was due. 'Week by week, they foretold a slight setback in business. When, by the summer of 1929, the setback had not appeared, the Society gave up and confessed error. Business might be good after all.' As late as November of that year, the Society argued that 'a severe depression is outside the range of probability. We are not facing protracted liquidation.' In Galbraith's laconic phrase, 'This view the Society reiterated until *it* was liquidated.'

Harvard was by no means the only Ivy League institution which failed to predict what was by far the deepest and most prolonged depression in American history. In the autumn of 1929, Professor Irving Fisher of Yale pronounced that 'stock prices have reached what looks like a permanently high plateau.' By the spring of 1930, the American stock market had already fallen sharply, and over the next couple of years went on to experience its most devastating collapse of all time.

Fisher was the most distinguished American economist of the early decades of this century. One of his many contributions was an article in the *Journal of the American Statistical Association* in 1925. In this, he himself argued that the business cycle is inherently unpredictable. If only he had borne his own words in mind in 1929. But Fisher's contention was a very serious one. He believed that movements over time in the volume of output were 'a composite of numerous elementary fluctuations, both cyclical and non-cyclical', and quoted approvingly from his contemporary Moore, who wrote that 'business cycles differ widely in duration, in intensity, in the sequence of their phases and in the relative prominence of their various phenomena.'

In such circumstances, it would be virtually impossible to distinguish data generated by such a system from data which was genuinely random in terms of its predictability. There are too many factors, and not enough data with which to identify their separate impacts.

In many ways, Fisher's world is very similar to that inhabited by our ants. Economic agents, whether individuals or companies, have their own rules of behaviour for making decisions, whatever these rules might be. But the overall effect of these rules, and how the individuals react to one another's behaviour, appears to produce an outcome which is very difficult to predict. In the same way, the ants follow rules of behaviour in deciding which food site to visit, and, unlike in the economy, we know exactly what these rules are. But the net outcome of the interactions between the ants is inherently uncertain and unpredictable.

In the economy, individuals and firms take decisions which lead to the ups and downs, the booms and recessions, of the business cycle. In the same way, the behaviour of the ants leads to fluctuations in the overall outcome, in this case the proportion of the colony visiting any one of the sites. The analogy between the business cycle and the world of the ants is an important one, and is taken up in much more detail in Chapters 8 and 9. Here we are simply concerned with the question of the predictability of the overall outcomes which arise from the behaviour of a multitude of individuals.

Despite the respectable background in economics which insists that successful short-term prediction of the overall economy is not feasible, economic policy in Western economies continues to be dominated by short-term economic forecasts. Responsibility for them varies from country to country depending upon the political structure, but in many European countries the finance minister pronounces from time to time on the likely growth in national output (GDP) over the next year, and the figure is eagerly dissected. According to political tastes, it is used as evidence either that prudent stewardship is paying off, or that the government and its ideas are as bankrupt as the economy.

At regular intervals, the minister may joust with the governor of the central bank to decide, for example, whether interest rates should be raised immediately in response to a forecast that in a year or two's time inflation will be slightly higher than it is now. Many other similar questions dominate political and economic debate. Will Italian public borrowing as a percentage of GDP be sufficiently low in 1997/98 to meet the Maastricht criteria?* Is the prolonged recession in Japan finally coming to an end? The list could go on and on.

For any particular year, a prediction may prove correct, an event which the forecaster concerned, whether in the public or private sector, is only too keen to highlight. But taken by itself, this has no more meaning than someone accurately predicting the outcome of a single roll of dice. A far better test is whether over a period of years – or a sequence of shakes of the dice – reasonable forecasts can be made. It is always possible to get things right purely by chance, but with even a small number of predictions over time, the probability of so doing drops rapidly towards zero. The odds, for example, of correctly guessing the results of just three successive shakes of a reliable dice are over 200 to 1 against, while for six successive correct guesses, the odds are over 40,000 to 1.

Forecasting is known to be difficult, especially, as cynics remark, when it concerns the future. The British Prime Minister, Tony Blair, inadvertently contributed to this debate during the 1997 election campaign. Asked by an interviewer to speculate on his chances of victory, Blair declined the offer politely, saying, 'I have never been in the business of making predictions, I am not now, and I never will be in that business.'

Even a cursory acquaintance with the evidence on the accuracy of macro-economic forecasts raises doubts as to their value. During 1997, for example, there were spectacular failures of prediction concerning the East Asian economies. In May of that year the International Monetary Fund (IMF) predicted a continuation of the enormous growth rates which those economies had experienced for a number of years: 7 per cent growth was projected for Thailand in 1998, 7.5 per cent for Indonesia and 8 per cent for Malaysia. By October, these had been revised down to 3.5, 6 and 6.5 per cent respectively. But by December the IMF was forecasting

---

* As this chapter is being revised, it has now been deemed by the European Commission to be sufficiently low, but only by dint of what can best be described, even charitably, as some creative accounting.

only 3 per cent growth for Malaysia and Indonesia, and zero for Thailand. And in the spring of 1998, the outlook is even worse again.

An example of a more systematic failure comes from the UK, where the average error made by the Treasury on one-year-ahead forecasts of GDP growth is around 1.5 per cent. This might seem small, until one remembers that the average *actual* growth rate over this period has been around 2 per cent a year. In other words, the typical forecast error has been almost the same size as the data itself. An average error which is so large relative to the actual series being forecast means that such projections have very little value. Suppose the forecast for next year is for the average 2 per cent growth rate. If it were wrong by just the average forecast error, in one direction the outcome would be a serious recession, with only 0.5 per cent growth, and in the other direction a mini-boom of 3.5 per cent expansion. But the true range of uncertainty is considerably wider than this. In some years in the past the forecast has been, by chance, nearly correct, with an error close to zero. So if there is an average error of 1.5 per cent over a period of time, errors significantly bigger than the average must be made in other years.

The UK is not alone in the inaccuracy of macro-economic forecasts. In the June 1993 OECD *Economic Outlook*, the forecasting record of the G7 governments – the United States, Japan, Germany, France, Italy, Canada and the UK – the IMF and the OECD itself was assessed over the period 1987–92. The accuracy of one-year-ahead forecasts for GDP growth and inflation were compared with the very simple prediction that next year's growth or inflation would be the same as this year's. This gave very poor forecasts, with large errors. But it was just as good as the forecasts which were actually made and, arguably, in the case of inflation, marginally better.

The problems of forecasting are not confined to official bodies, nor to any particular theory of how the economy operates. All approaches, whether governmental or private, Keynesian or monetarist, have done equally badly. From time to time an institution may appear to perform well, but in the longer run there are no unambiguous rankings of accuracy, a point which was emphasized in a major survey of macro-economic forecasting in the *Economic Journal* by Ken Wallis in 1989, the validity of which has not been altered by subsequent experience.

The question of the predictability of data series such as GDP growth or the rate of inflation can now be examined rigorously, using techniques which have been developed during the past decade in the discipline of non-linear signal processing. My aim in the discussion below is to try to illustrate these ideas in a non-technical way.

Many people are familiar with the idea that radio signals can be displayed in graphical form on a screen, with peaks and troughs charting the relative intensity of the volume of the signal being picked up. Given the recent proliferation of hi-tech hospital dramas on television, perhaps even more will recognize that the pulsating rhythm of a heart can also be represented graphically on a screen.

Figure 1.1 on p. 6 plotted the variations over time in the proportion of the ant colony visiting one of the food sites. Figure 6.1 plots a different set of fluctuations, namely the movements in the quarterly growth rate of GDP in the UK over the period 1955–95.

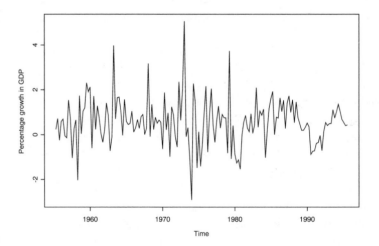

FIGURE 6.1   UK real quarterly growth 1955–95

Analytically, these seemingly disparate examples can all be thought of in the same way: they each chart the fluctuations over time of particular processes, be they radio signals, heart beats, ants or the economic cycle.

Confronted by such a plot of data, a researcher enjoined with the task of forecasting its future movements will usually try to obtain some mathematical expression which replicates the key features of the available data, and then use it as the basis for forecasts. Exactly how this is done, and the forms of expression which might be tried, are not our immediate concerns. Our concern is whether or not, *in principle*, a reasonably accurate mathematical representation of the available data can be obtained. This is the issue addressed by signal-processing techniques. They are not attempting to build a specific mathematical model of any particular data series, but to answer two questions which arise prior to this task.

First, how successful is *any* model-building approach likely to be? The techniques deal with this question by breaking down any given set of data fluctuations over time into two components: those which have a reasonable degree of regularity, and those which are purely random.

The reception for radio programmes, especially those which cater for minority tastes, is not always good. One can be listening to a piece of music only to have it interrupted, irritatingly, by various hisses and squeals. If such a sequence were plotted over time, signal-processing techniques could identify the proportion of the sequence which contained recognizable patterns, and which could therefore be presumed to be genuine music (the 'signal'), and the proportion which was simply interference (the 'noise'). To pursue the model-building analogy, the techniques would not indicate in any way who the composer might be, but would identify that a proportion of the overall transmission appeared to have sufficient pattern to indicate that it was a piece of music (with the exception, of course, of people such as Stockhausen and John Cage) rather than being random emissions of noise.

The existence of a relatively high degree of 'signal' to 'noise' is a necessary condition which must hold for reasonable forecasts of the relevant data series to be made. A series dominated by noise is very similar to a purely random series, which, by definition, cannot be consistently forecast with any degree of accuracy.

The second question dealt with by signal-processing techniques can be described more succinctly. While the first considers the ratio of signal to noise in any given data set, the second gives information on the maximum number of factors which contribute to the signal component of the data. Again, it must be emphasized that the technique does not tell us what these factors might be, but simply how many of them are required in order to get a good representation of the signal component.

We might think, to try to illustrate the point, of a skilled big-game hunter, or, more likely these days, an expert conservationist, examining the tracks of a pride of lions over a dusty bit of ground. The pack leader, being bigger and heavier than the rest, leaves the deepest and best defined footprints, while the babies, who contribute little to the functioning of the pack, leave very small, light ones. To understand the movements of the pack, we only need to follow the best footprints. But if they are all very light and faint, our task becomes very difficult.

Some appreciation of the technique can be illustrated by the remarkable system of equations developed by the meteorologist Edward Lorenz in the early 1960s. Without exaggeration, this system stimulated the development of the entire modern literature on chaos theory, even though it took some years following its publication for its significance to be recognized. The distinguishing feature of chaotic systems is that very small initial differences eventually make an enormous difference to the outcome. For our purposes, however, the important point is not the eventual outcome of a set of equations for a chaotic system, but the early parts of it. In the short term, two solutions obtained by starting off with slightly different values for the variables will be very similar. They will move further and further apart over time, but, in their initial stages, they will stay close together. An implication of this is that someone who knew the details of the equations but who only knew approximately where the system was starting from, would nevertheless be able, for a short time, to make reasonable forecasts of the variables in the system. Eventually, the forecasts would have enormous errors, but initially they would be pretty accurate.

The fact that reasonable short-term forecasts can be made in a chaotic system may seem surprising, particularly when Figure 6.2 is inspected. This plots the typical movements over time of one of the three variables in the Lorenz system of equations. It is obvious that the movements are erratic, indeed, spectacularly so. Confronted by this chart, with no knowledge of the equations which generated it, one might despair that the series could ever be predicted with any reasonable degree of accuracy.

But plotting the same data in a different way in Figure 6.3 gives quite a

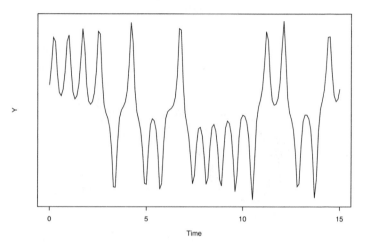

FIGURE 6.2 A chaotic series from the Lorenz system

different picture, in all senses of the word. Figure 6.3 is obtained in the following way. Take a value of the variable y any point in time. Then read off the value of y in the previous period, and of y in the period before that. This gives us three values for y – at time t, in the period immediately before t, and in the period two periods before. These can be plotted as a single point in the three-dimensional chart shown in Figure 6.3, whose axes are y in the current period, y in the previous period, and y two periods ago. By connecting each of the plotted points in sequence, the distinctive butterfly wings pattern emerges in Figure 6.3. Contrary to first impressions, the data has a definite structure.

In many ways, the essence of non-linear signal processing is to try to plot the data in a different way to see if its underlying structure can be revealed, as the contrast between Figures 6.2 and 6.3 shows. (Of course, these charts are merely illustrative of the results obtained when the heavy-duty maths is actually used.) These techniques cannot, however, reveal structure where none exists. Figure 6.4, for example, plots a purely random set of data in exactly the same way as the Lorenz data in Figure 6.3. By definition, such data lacks any structure, as is obvious from Figure 6.4. Even the application of full-blown signal-processing

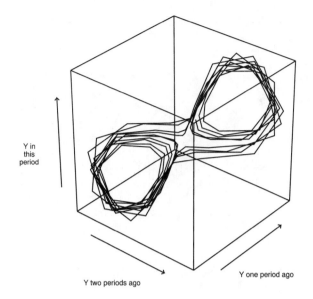

FIGURE 6.3 Three-dimensional plot of chaotic data from Figure 6.2

techniques to the series fails to reveal any consistent patterns.

Figures 6.3 and 6.4 can be thought of as templates for the two extremes of the potential predictability of a series of data. The data plotted in the former clearly has a great deal of structure. Despite the fact that the series is chaotic, the plot shows that *in principle* reasonable short-term forecasts could be made. The system does occasionally switch dramatically from one wing of the butterfly to the next. But, most of the time, the system stays on the same wing, and hence the point where it is at any given time provides useful information about where it is likely to be in the immediate future. In contrast, the data set out in Figure 6.4 is spread out in a haphazard way around the chart, with little indication of any pattern existing between what happens in any given period and in the subsequent periods. What happens now tells us very little about what is likely to happen, and so reasonable forecasts can never be made.

We can venture back into the world of our ants, and see what happens when the signal-processing technique is applied to their behaviour. While Figure 6.4 uses data which by construction is purely random, our ants

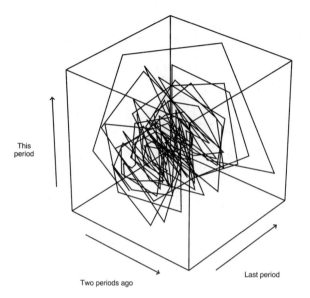

This
period

Two periods ago

Last period

FIGURE 6.4 Three-dimensional plot of a random series

follow rules of behaviour, which we can write down in a straightforward way. An ant either visits the same site it did previously, switches sites of its own accord, or is influenced by other ants to switch sites. But we are never certain about what any individual ant will do, for there is only a probability, not a certainty, that at any point an ant will follow a particular rule.

Figure 1.1 showed the proportion of the ant colony which visits one of the two possible sites at any point in time. Figure 6.5 plots this data in three dimensions.

The ant data spreads out and fills the chart in an apparently un-structured, unsystematic way. Changes in the proportion of ants visiting a given site are in general of no value in predicting what will happen in the immediate future.

The analysis of macro–economic time-series data shows that its degree of structure, or rather the lack of it, corresponds much more to the examples in Figures 6.4 and 6.5 than it does to Figure 6.3. This is shown clearly in Figure 6.6, a three-dimensional plot of the UK GDP growth

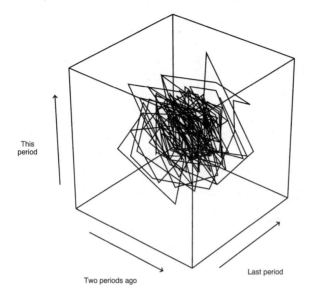

FIGURE 6.5 Three-dimensional plot of the ants model

data which is plotted over time in the conventional way in Figure 6.1.*

The results of Figure 6.6 are typical of a wide range of macro-economic data series in European countries. Although this may well not be apparent by inspecting the charts, there is usually a small degree of structure in the data, so the results are not identical to those of a purely random series, but it is insufficient to allow forecasts of any reasonable degree of accuracy to be carried out systematically over time. Consumer spending, for example – a data series which has attracted enormous attention from economists over the years – looks very similar to GDP when analysed in this way.

Inflation appears at first sight to have a strong element of structure, but on closer inspection this turns out merely to reflect the degree of inertia in this series. Many of the factors which contribute to next period's inflation – such as this period's wage increases, which then become next period's

* Economic forecasts are usually reported for the average growth over a year rather than for each individual quarter. But, obviously, growth over the course of a year is simply the sum of the growth in each of the four quarters. So problems of predicting quarterly growth necessarily extend to annual forecasts. This point is expanded, using simple arithmetic, in Appendix 1.

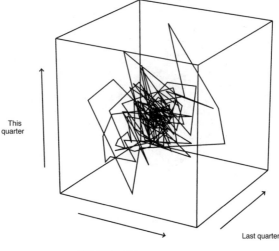

This
quarter

Last quarter

Two quarters ago

FIGURE 6.6 Three-dimensional plot of UK real GDP growth

labour costs – are decided during the current period at the current rate of inflation. Not surprisingly, therefore, inflation does not move about a great deal in the immediate short term. But over a time period as short as a quarter, the *change* in inflation has very little underlying structure at all. In other words, once allowance is made for the short-term inertia which exists in the inflation data, it becomes just as unpredictable as GDP.

The American economy is a partial, but obviously important, exception to the general rule about the lack of structure and hence lack of predictability of macro-economic data series. Figure 6.7 plots the quarterly growth in post-war US real GNP* on the same basis as British GDP in Figure 6.6. Beauty is always in the eye of the beholder, and to some readers both charts may simply look like a ball of wool with which the cat has been playing. But there is rather more shape to the American chart, with more clearly discernible systematic loops, than there is with the British.

---

* There are some minor differences between GNP (Gross National Product) and GDP (Gross Domestic Product). For the European economies, in practice these are so trivial that the two are almost the same series, and by custom and practice GDP has become the series which is monitored.

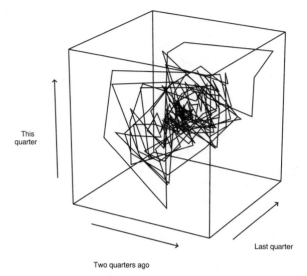

This
quarter

Last quarter

Two quarters ago

FIGURE 6.7 Three-dimensional plot of US real GNP growth

Even so, the contrast with Figure 6.3, in which the structure is
transparent, is striking. Figure 6.7 tells us (or, rather, the underlying
maths does) that a thoughtful and intelligent forecaster ought to be able to
have some success at predicting the short-term movements in the overall
output of the United States economy, but that his or her record will be
very far from perfect. Curiously, the only institution whose record
matches this description in recent years is the Federal Reserve. The vast
panoply of private-sector forecasters in the United States exhibit a
catalogue of failure. Indeed, in a systematic comparison published early in
1997 for the National Bureau of Economic Research, the economists
Christina and David Romer concluded that 'the commercial forecasters
would simply do better if they could discard their own forecasts and use
those of the Federal Reserve'.

The policy conclusions of all this are rather strong. A great deal of
economic policy in the West since the war has been and still is conducted
on the basis of short-term forecasts of the economy. Governments try to
anticipate the movements of the economy over the course of the business

cycle and to take action to correct any adverse consequences which would arise if such predictions were accurate.

But governments, and those who advise them on these issues, are suffering from the delusion of control. Over a period of years, it is not possible in the current state of scientific knowledge to make short-term forecasts with any reasonable degree of accuracy. In any single year, a forecast may prove by chance to be correct, but over time large errors in individual years will inevitably be made. This is the case even in the United States, where we have just seen that some degree of predictability can be achieved.

Some may feel that the conclusion is too strong, arising as it does from the application of an esoteric mathematical technique whose intricacies are rather impenetrable to the non-specialist.* But it is entirely consistent with the actual macro-economic forecasting record in the West over the past twenty or thirty years. The averages and the values of the forecast errors which have been made are very similar to the actual data series themselves.

From a purely empirical standpoint, this suggests very strongly that such forecasts have little value and certainly do not provide a basis which can justify the enormous amount of effort and attention devoted by governments to these activities. Non-linear signal processing provides a powerful explanation of why forecasts have been so bad, and why the record is highly unlikely to improve in the near future.

This conclusion is valid regardless of the ideological or methodological view of what drives the economy in the short term, through the fluctuations of the business cycle. It arises from deep properties of macro-economic data, which in turn suggests a view of economic behaviour which is much closer to our ants model than it is to conventional theory.

---

* Conventional forecasters might try to offer a defence based on the distinction between so-called uni-variate and multi-variate models. This is dealt with, in non-technical terms, in Appendix 1.

CHAPTER 7

A Quantitative Quagmire

Conventional forecasters base what they believe will happen to the economy – to growth, inflation, unemployment and so on – on rules of behaviour. They spend a great deal of time searching for rules to describe what determines, say, the total amount which individuals spend, or how much firms export.

Econometricians – the term for those who try to build mathematical models of the economy using statistical techniques – construct the individual equations expressing the rules of behaviour, which form the basis of their models of the economy. The amount spent by consumers, for example, will obviously depend in part on their incomes. But a host of other factors may come into play, such as interest rates, reflecting the ease or otherwise of borrowing, or rising unemployment, which might deter people from spending on large items for fear of losing their own jobs in the near future.

The abysmal record of actual forecasts which econometricians have made using conventionally defined rules appears not to deter them at all. Rather like Tom in his endless and fruitless pursuit of Jerry, they are ever-hopeful, that, one day, with a bit of a refinement of specification here or a bit of new technique there, they will achieve the success which has so far eluded them. But, as the previous chapter indicates, the problems run much deeper.

Our ants behave according to specified rules. At any one time, an ant has a choice about *which* rule of behaviour to follow – to revisit the same site, or to switch sites. And the rule which a particular ant follows may change from period to period. But the vision of the world offered by conventional economists is fundamentally different from that of the world of our ants. Economists are looking for rules which in principle *never* change. Their whole motivation is to find equations – rules – which describe particular aspects of behaviour, and which stay the same for long periods of time. They see the economy as a machine and not as a living organism.

Further, the probability of any particular ant switching its behaviour and choosing a different rule depends directly upon what other ants do. As we have emphasized many times, this is not the case in the standard economic approach. People are assumed to have fixed tastes and preferences. The actions of others can only alter their behaviour indirectly. A firm which sacks some workers, for example, causes them to spend less money. But their basic preferences and behaviour are not changed: in choosing what to spend when made unemployed, the fixed rule applies, and the new level of their income is slotted into the formula.

An appreciation of the properties of our ants model leads us to realize that the conventional techniques of economists will never allow them to find their Holy Grail of unchanging rules which describe the behaviour of the economy. It is not that the behaviour of individuals is entirely random. In the case of the ants, there is a very clear set of rules which they follow. But it is the occasional random switches between different rules which makes the system as a whole – the behaviour of the colony – effectively impossible to predict. Even if we knew for certain the rules which the ants followed, we could never produce consistently accurate forecasts.

In order for short-term intervention in the economy to be successful, as Milton Friedman argued over forty years ago, governments need to be able to have access to reasonably reliable forecasts. If the economy is going to boom in a year's time, and if as a result inflation will rise, a government might want to try to start slowing it down now by putting up interest rates or raising taxes. Equally, if the economy is likely to move into a recession, a government will usually want to boost economic activity. But, as we have seen, forecasts of the economy even just one year ahead are inherently extremely uncertain.

And in order to be able to make the short-term future better than it would otherwise have been, governments need a further piece of information: they require a reasonably exact understanding of what the effects of various policy measures are on the economy. There would be little point in trying to exercise short-term control over the economy, by altering interest rates, say, if the effects of doing this on growth, inflation, unemployment and so on were not really understood. It is to this latter question which we now turn.

Governments in the West have at their disposal a vast range of policy instruments with which to influence the economy: changes in public spending, in income-tax rates, sales-tax rates, interest rates and so on. Undoubtedly, changes in such factors do have an effect on the economy. The problem is that estimates of both the size and the timing of their impacts vary enormously.

The rules which econometricians believe they have discovered are used not only to make predictions, but also to offer advice to governments on policy. So, equipped with a rule which purports to describe the factors which make people spend in the shops, economists pronounce that changes in income-tax rates will make people increase or decrease their spending by an amount indicated by the rule.

In the large* models of the economy which econometricians build, the various individual rules, or equations, are connected in complicated ways. For example, the total amount spent by consumers might depend, amongst other things, on unemployment and how fast it is changing. But unemployment itself may well be determined in part by how much consumers are spending. The individual equations are constructed separately, and then fitted together into the model of the entire economy. It is almost like the task of building a medieval cathedral. Each separate piece of stone is carefully crafted, and then is slotted into the edifice as a whole, and the way in which the stones are connected produces the overall effect.

Once fitted together and the connections established, the models can be used to trace the full effects of a change in government policy, effects which obviously extend beyond their immediate impact in any individual equation. A reduction in, say, sales taxes such as Value Added Tax or excise duties on alcohol, can be expected to lead to an increase in consumer spending. This in turn, in our hypothesized model, brings about a reduction in unemployment, which itself generates a further rise in consumer spending, and so on.

The process just described is the basic principle of the famous Keynesian multiplier. Writing in the 1930s, Keynes advocated public

---

* An alert modeller would no doubt say at this point that their models now are smaller than they used to be. This is true, for at one time many had the best part of a thousand equations. But they are still big by any objective standards.

works as a solution to the high levels of unemployment which gripped the Western economies. A great aesthete, Keynes would probably have preferred that works of art such as cathedrals should be built, but he recognized that the more mundane occupation of getting the unemployed to dig holes in the ground and then fill them in would serve the purpose just as well.

Keynes led the group of economists at Cambridge in the early 1930s who worked out the concept of the multiplier – the idea that the initial impact of, say, an increase in public spending or a cut in taxes would be multiplied as its influence spread through the economy and the various interconnections and feedbacks operated.

Keynes himself, despite, or more probably because of, his own extensive training in mathematics, looked with disdain on attempts to quantify the economy by statistical means. On this occasion, however, he did venture the opinion that in the context of the British economy of the 1930s, the multiplier might lie between 2 and 3. In other words, an initial increase in public spending of £1 million would eventually lead to an increase in total spending and output of somewhere between £2 and 3 million.

There is far more to Keynes's economics than the multiplier, but it is this which has been the object of intensive study by econometricians, particularly in the past thirty years or so as developments in computer technology have made it far easier to use the various statistical techniques which are needed to build the models. And, although sixty years have elapsed since Keynes first presented his idea to the wider world, no consensus has emerged on the size of the multiplier.

The problem is not just the size of the multiplier, but its *sign*. Some models give the result that, once all the various interconnections in the economy have been activated, an increase in public spending eventually leads to overall spending being lower than it would otherwise have been. In other words, the multiplier is *negative*!

This seemingly paradoxical result can arise because of the complicated connections between the financial sector and the rest of the economy. The exact details need not concern us. But increases in public spending unaccompanied by increases in taxes require the government to meet the bill in one way or another. The authorities could borrow money or they could simply print some new money. Either way, there are impacts on financial markets, on factors such as interest rates and exchange rates. If additional government spending led to higher interest rates, say, the depressing effect of the latter on the economy could outweigh the positive effect of the former.

A good illustration of the lack of consensus on the size of the multiplier is the results of an exercise published in 1997, financed by the British Economic and Social Research Council. The five leading, orthodox macro-economic modelling teams were required to ask their model what would be the effects of a number of policy changes, such as increasing public expenditure by a specified amount, or trying to achieve a specific reduction in inflation, and the results were compared.

All the models agreed that the initial impact of an increase in government expenditure on spending and output in the economy as a whole was positive, though small. But once all the complicated inter-relationships in the models were allowed to feed through, not only the size but the sign of the multiplier was different. Another example from the same exercise was the answers to the question as to what would happen if policies were adjusted to reduce inflation by one percentage point. Two of the models said that this would eventually reduce output as well, and increase unemployment by as much as half a million. But the other three said output would rise and unemployment fall.

A great deal of the debate on economic policy, both in government and in the media, focuses on the short term. But it is based on illusions – the illusion that is possible to make, on a consistent basis, forecasts which have a reasonable degree of accuracy; and on the resulting illusion that governments can use these forecasts to successfully control short-term developments in the economy. Governments, like the rest of us, have a great deal to learn from our ants.

In the basic ants model, there is no possibility of analysing the effects of factors which are thought to have a *systematic* influence on behaviour. In Chapters 3 and 4 when we discussed the issues of crime and the family, we extended the primary principles of the ants model to incorporate such factors. And this analysis provides an important insight into why the conventional approaches in economic modelling produce consistently contradictory results.

The impact of a given change in any particular factor, whether it is the rate of income tax or the severity of the criminal justice system, can vary substantially depending upon the exact circumstances in which the change is made. This is the whole logic of our complex systems approach. As we saw with the crime model, small changes usually have small effects, as we would expect logically. But occasionally, depending upon where we start from, they can have larger ones, and sometimes very large ones. Further, two quite different levels of crime can be associated with exactly the same values for the factors which are thought to cause crime.

These subtleties of behaviour are effectively absent from the machine-like conventional economic models. Occasionally, modellers do try to allow for them in a piecemeal sort of way, as add-ons to their basic structures. But in fact they are a deep-seated and integral part of the structure of how the economy really operates.

Thinking of the economy or society as a complex, living system rather than a machine has important implications for the conduct of policy. In particular, the impossibility of short-term precision and control means that governments in general should do less rather than more. Persuading politicians and their supportive bureaucracies that they should follow this precept is not easy. Indeed, it is one of the most difficult implications for practical men and women to accept, reared as they have been on the check-list mentality of policy. But it is a clear implication, which arises time and time again in a wide range of contexts.

The attention paid to short-term forecasting, and the delusion of control which it offers, diverts both resources and debate away from more important matters. Governments *do* have a powerful influence, for good or for ill, on the overall structural framework in which the economy operates. It is this which should be the focus of discussion rather than the frenzy of interventionism which passes for policy most of the time. Less can be more.

The arguments in Europe over the Maastricht convergence criteria illustrate the extent to which this insidious short-termism – the true 'short-term' disease – can detract from the real issues. To qualify for European Monetary Union, an economy must exhibit convergence with others on three short-term criteria, over very short, specified periods: the inflation rate, and the sizes of both public borrowing and the outstanding stock of public debt relative to the size of the economy. The simple fact is that, in the current state of scientific knowledge, it is not possible to predict whether in the future in Germany, say, the public sector deficit as a share of GDP or inflation will meet the arbitrary criteria in any given year.

We do know, however, that Germany has been devoted to low inflation and sound finance for many years. The whole of its social and political fabric has been developed around this goal. The economy has had a long time to adapt and, despite the firm commitment to a strong currency and consequent over-valuation of the mark, Germany has been able to maintain reasonable economic growth in the difficult overall environment of the past twenty years.

Countries such as Italy or Spain have not as yet 'converged' with the German economy. They are judged to have done so because of the purely short-term criteria which have been used. Monetary union is a policy of great power and ruthlessness. For instance, for much of the time since monetary union in the sixteenth century, the Welsh economy has depended, and still depends today, on capital flows and fiscal transfers from the stronger English one. On any set of broader, structural criteria, the Mediterranean economies are simply not in a fit state to be linked with Germany's without large and sustained fiscal transfers. Short-term forecasts and short-term criteria mutually reinforce each other and offer the illusion that it all makes sense.

We can think of the immediate post-war years as a good illustration of the benefits which arise whenever governments get the overall policy framework right. It is this, rather than a host of specific measures, which really matters.

After the war, there was enormous supply-side potential for growth. In Europe in particular, personal consumer spending had been rationed severely for a number of years. There was a pent-up backlog of demand which could, and did, translate itself into a willingness to buy almost anything which was produced. Companies knew this, so their overall level of optimism was high. They had the confidence to invest, which further boosted orders and growth, and fed back positively to confidence itself. And on the Continent, a great deal of the capital stock of industry had been destroyed and needed replacing. The skills of the workforce had remained intact, and in many ways were enhanced by the experience of war-time production. Everything was in place on the supply side to generate the very rapid rates of growth which were observed in the 1950s and for much of the 1960s.

Yet things could have gone seriously wrong. The initial transition of the European countries out of their war economies was hampered by a shortage of finance, and notably of foreign exchange to pay for imports. The extraordinary generosity and far-sightedness of the American Marshall Plan was a key factor in overcoming this potentially serious hurdle. Perhaps even more importantly, recipients of funds from the Plan had to commit themselves to the principle of the market economy, and to dismantle the extensive planning and control structures assembled during the war. Such a framework can mobilize resources successfully during a crisis, but, as the experience of the Soviet bloc shows only too clearly, eventually proves stultifying.

The international world order could have retreated, as it did so disastrously after the First World War, into protectionism and monetary disorder. But again, mainly due to America's ability to impose its will, a process of dismantling trade barriers was set in motion, and the Bretton Woods agreement brought order to the world money markets.

It is relatively easy to look back at the past and see the successful episodes that set the longer-term framework in which economies operate. It is much harder, and the real challenge, to think about what governments can do now. But it is possible to make constructive suggestions by stepping back from the frenzy of short-term policy-making.

An illustration is given in Figure 7.1. Since the mid-1970s, average growth in European economies over a number of cycles has been distinctly lower than it was in the 1950s and 1960s, falling from an annual average of almost 5 per cent from 1960 to 1973, to just over 2 per cent in the two decades since 1974. In Japan, the fall has been even greater, from over 9 per cent a year on average to just over 3 per cent. The United States has been relatively immune, but even here growth slowed from around 3.5 per cent a year to 2.5 per cent.

Figure 7.1 plots the change in average growth rates for each of the main Western economies, comparing the 1974–95 period with that of

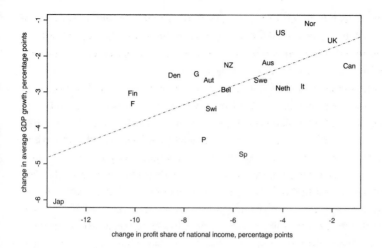

FIGURE 7.1 Change in average GDP growth and profit share: OECD economies, 1974–95 on 1960–73

1960–73, and the change in the average share of profits in total national income between those periods.

The interpretation is as follows. Japan is marked on the chart in the lower left-hand corner. The axis on the left tells us that the change in the average annual growth rate in Japan was around 6 per cent – as mentioned above, growth fell from over 9 per cent a year to just over 3 per cent, a fall of 6 per cent. The axis at the bottom indicates that the average share of profits in national income in Japan fell by 12 per cent. This does not mean that profits in Japan fell in terms of their absolute size, but that they grew much less quickly than the Japanese economy as a whole. The share of profits in total income fell, not profits themselves.

There is a very clear negative relationship between the change in profitability and the change in growth. The more profits as a share of total income fell, the bigger was the drop in the average annual growth rate between 1974 and 1995. In the top right of the chart are Norway, the United Kingdom and the United States. Growth in these countries fell on average by only 1.4 per cent, compared to an average of 2.9 per cent for the other sixteen Western economies in the chart. And the fall in profitability of these economies was much lower. (The experience of Norway owes a great deal to the discovery of North Sea oil, for the finds have been very large in comparison to the overall size of the Norwegian economy.)

In part, lower growth itself tends to depress profitability, but much of the longer-term erosion of profitability took place in the late 1960s and early 1970s, so the 1974–95 period as a whole experienced distinctly lower profitability than had previously been the case. The chart is not conclusive proof that a revival of profitability is required in order to raise the longer-term growth rate of the Western economies. But it certainly suggests that this is a policy guideline which merits close examination.

Another example of the advantages of taking a broader, systemic view is provided by current anxieties about inflation. Central banks throughout the West, and especially in Europe, are paranoid about a resurrection of inflation. If economic growth becomes too strong, if unemployment falls too much, inflation might get out of control. This way of thinking has dominated the central banks of continental Europe for the past fifteen years. Keep credit tight and screw down public spending for fear of inflation. Little wonder that unemployment in Europe is now higher than at any time since the 1930s.

But what is all the fuss about? In the United States, except in the black inner cities, there is now full employment. Yet inflation is low, between 2 and 3 per cent, the sort of rates which America had during the 1950s and 1960s when there also was full employment. In Britain, since 1993 the economy has expanded and unemployment has almost halved. But inflation has actually fallen.*

So full employment in the US and a dramatic fall in unemployment in the UK have *not* led to increases in inflation. Yet British and European economic policy remains dominated by the view that low unemployment *does* automatically lead to higher inflation. A great deal of sophisticated mathematical, statistical work is done within the crabbed confines of conventional economics to try to establish this result – without much success, for very often no sooner has a rule been obtained than it is contradicted by what happens next.

But the basic thinking behind the idea is that of the elementary free-market rules of supply and demand. If the demand for a product

---

* Using the broader and more relevant measure published in the national accounts, rather than the narrow one of media headlines.

increases, its price will rise. So if the demand for labour increases – more jobs, less unemployment – the price of labour rises. And since the price of labour is the wage or salary, and these make up a large part of employers' costs, as wages rise, prices will too. Cost increases are passed on by firms.

Again, we need the wider context to understand what is going on. The same values for variables which might be thought to cause inflation can be associated in different historical contexts with quite different values for the rate of inflation – in exactly the same way that different crime rates can be associated with an identical set of factors such as social and economic conditions and the nature of the criminal justice system.

If we take a conventional approach and only take data from a small part of the total set of information available, such as the experience of the past twenty years or so, we might be able to convince ourselves that lower unemployment leads to higher inflation, and vice versa. But the broader approach tells us that we have now switched into an entirely different part of the chart, as it were. In the crime example in Chapter 3, the really important thing in determining the level of crime is which of the two solid lines we are on, rather than our exact position on either of these lines. In the same way, we can think of inflation being in one of two 'regimes': high or low.

From a broad historical perspective, we can see that the capitalist market economies *normally* deliver either zero or very low inflation. It is the period of the 1970s and 1980s which is most unusual, and whose nearness distorts our perspective.

During world wars, we can see how supply and demand do lead to inflation. National survival is at stake, the economy is at absolutely full belt, and bottle-necks abound. But if we strip out the war periods, in 1950, in both Britain and America, the price level was no higher than it was in 1850 – zero inflation over the course of a century. And during the 1950s and 1960s, with full employment, inflation was only 2 to 3 per cent.

What are the factors at work which are keeping inflation low now across the world? In part, there is a self-reinforcing process at work. People and institutions adapt to the prevailing regime and alter their behaviour in the light of how others behave. Pensions, for example, were not indexed automatically to inflation until the 1970s, when inflation really was high. In the same way, low inflation becomes accepted – outside government circles, that is.

Commodity prices are weak. This causes problems for the incomes of producer countries, but keeps pressure off prices in the West. We also see very rapid falls in the prices of new technology products. Video recorders, computers, even the old television, have seen enormous falls in their prices. In addition, many low-value-added sectors of the economy, from traditional manufacturing to routine computer programming work, face new competition from Asia. This keep prices down.

Perhaps most importantly, some really major consumer markets have become close to saturation. The car industry is the biggest one of all. For almost the whole of this century, car manufacturers could rely collectively on the demand for their product rising faster than the economy as a whole. More and more households were acquiring cars for the first time; now this process has ended. There is still scope for expansion in the second-car market, and people still need to replace cars. But the proportion of households in the West with a car is now almost as high as it will ever get.

In these circumstances, manufacturers are compelled to compete much more on price. They cannot rely on automatic growth in their market. And the more attuned customers become to price, the harder and harder it becomes to push prices higher.

The wider perspective tells us we are back in the normal, low-inflation regime typical of the history of capitalism. There will still be fluctuations over the course of the business cycle, but sustained reductions in unemployment will make little difference to the average rate of inflation. And the actual experience of the 1990s confirms this view. Fear of inflation is really an urban myth *de nos jours*.

Whether it is monetary union, economic growth, inflation or whatever, these broader, systemic perspectives provide the kind of evidence which governments should be looking for if they are to have a beneficial and positive effect through their management of the economy. Governments do matter and their actions affect us all, for better or for worse. But it is time to stop pretending that they know what they are doing when they fiddle with the short-term economic controls. The basic implications of the behaviour of our ants, of the inherent unpredictability of short-term outcomes for the system as a whole, apply nowhere more strongly than here.

CHAPTER 8

Ups and Downs

The short-run fluctuations in economic growth discussed in the previous two chapters are perhaps the most striking feature of the capitalist market economies of the West. Any system of thought which purports to understand the economy must be able to offer a reasonable explanation of the phenomenon.

The difficulties of short-term prediction and control of the economy are clear, and the world of our ants exhibits very similar properties. The first part of this chapter describes briefly two further fundamental empirical aspects of the business cycle, and notes additional parallels with the properties of our ants model. But most of the chapter is devoted to a discussion of some of the more cerebral, theoretical attempts which have been made in economics to understand the business cycle, in contrast to the number-crunching efforts of econometricians discussed in the previous chapters. In particular, we examine the problems which the existence of the business cycle causes for orthodox theory, not least for the currently fashionable 'real business cycle' theory.

From time to time, politicians pronounce that the business cycle is dead. This is, invariably, due to the brilliance of the economic policies which they have pursued. But, as so often with their utterances, the content proves to be one of pure delusion. Figure 8.1 is an example of the permanent existence of such cycles; it plots the annual rate of growth of real national output* per head in the United States over the period 1871–1997. And the experience of America is entirely typical of the Western capitalist economies as whole.

The most striking feature of the annual rate of growth of American

---

* An important point to note is that the terms 'national output' and 'national income' can be used interchangeably. In the national economic accounts, they are separate measures of the same thing, namely the size of the economy.

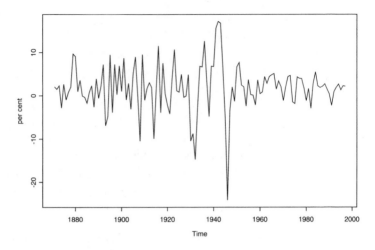

FIGURE 8.1 Annual percentage change in real per capita US national output
1871–1997

national income is that it is always changing. It is never the same from one
year to the next.

The average over this whole period has been clearly positive, at just
under 2 per cent a year. But around this average there are persistent, and
sometimes dramatic, fluctuations. The falls in the Great Depression in the
early 1930s were admittedly quite exceptional, as were the reductions in
output in the immediate aftermath of the Second World War as military
production was curtailed. But even in a stable environment such as that of
the peacetime United States, sharp movements can occur. From the early
1950s to date, there have been years when American output has fallen by
3 per cent, and years when it has expanded by as much as 6 per cent.

A second property of these business cycles is that they do not appear to
exhibit very much regularity either in their duration or in the size of their
movements from the trough of the recession to the peak of the next boom.
In technical terms, the former is referred to as the 'period' of the cycle
and the latter as the 'amplitude'. Even by inspecting the chart, it is clear
that whatever patterns might exist in the data alter over time. The
amplitude of the post-war data, for example, is obviously different from
that between the wars, which in turn differs from, say, the pre-1900 data.

This point was established very clearly by one of the first, and certainly one of the most distinguished, systematic studies of the economic statistics of the business cycle. In 1946 Burns and Mitchell of the National Bureau of Economic Research in the United States published a very detailed description of the history of all American business cycles to that date. Their conclusions have not really been altered by the enormous amount of work which has been subsequently carried out in this area. They stated that 'the sequence of changes is recurrent but not periodic; in duration cycles vary from more than one year to ten or twelve years; they are not divisible into shorter cycles of similar character with amplitudes approximating their own.'

The patterns in Figure 8.1 are by no means identical quantitatively to those in Figure 1.1, which plots the behaviour of our ants as they move from site to site. But they seem to share some qualitative aspects. For one thing, the data plotted in both charts is in a constant state of change, never settling down at a fixed value. Further, periods of *relative* stability are punctuated by large, rapid movements.

In other words, on the face of it, the principles of ant behaviour may have something to offer in terms of understanding the business cycle. But this, as all the best melodramas would put it, is to anticipate.

Attempts to account for the existence of business cycles have been a key theme in economic theory for the past two hundred years. In the first half of the nineteenth century, commentators tried to locate the source of the oscillations within the economy itself. In the jargon of the present day, they regarded cycles as being endogenous, or within the economic system. Subsequent economic orthodoxy sees them as exogenous, or outside the economy.

Of course, arguments about the nature of cycles long predate the development of modern economics. For example, one of the Fathers of the early Church, Origen, proposed a theory of Redemption in which the soul fluctuated between Heaven and Hell – a suggestion sternly denounced as heresy by Augustine, who would obviously have empathized with orthodox economics, for he specifically denied the existence of such endogenous cycles.

The amplitude of business cycles in the early decades of industrialization in Britain and other parts of Northern Europe does appear to have been particularly large. The violence of these movements was such that it features extensively in contemporary literature. In Mrs Gaskell's *North and South*, for example, one of the central characters is Thornton, the local mill-owner. He feels no pity for the workers during recessions, when unemployment is high and wages are forced down almost below basic subsistence levels. But he himself subsequently faces ruin during another massive cyclical downturn in the economy.

The great classical economists writing in the first half of the nineteenth century were fascinated by the new phenomenon of industrial capitalism, of rapid and unprecedented change and growth. Outside the discipline of economics, the name of David Ricardo is entirely unknown. But within the subject, this immensely wealthy English stockbroker is regarded as a true titan of thought.

It was by no means clear to someone like Ricardo, writing in the first two decades of the nineteenth century, that growth was a new and permanent feature of society. It appeared just as plausible that a sharp downturn in the economy might not be temporary, but would bring growth to a halt. Ricardo identified the potential for this within the labour market: 'There cannot be accumulated in a country any amount of capital which cannot be employed productively, until wages rise so high . . . and so little consequently remains for the profits of stock, that the motive for accumulation ceases. When the profits of stock are high, men will have a motive to accumulate.' In other words, the possibility existed that the outcome of bargaining over wages could lead to profits being too low for any further investment to take place, and hence growth would cease.

Writing some thirty years later, Marx effectively formalized Ricardo's views into a theory of business cycles. During an economic boom, the demand for labour rises, and unemployment falls, or, as Marx would have it, the 'reserve army of labour' is depleted. This causes wages to rise faster than the economy as a whole, and hence leads to a fall in profits. As a result, investment in new capital equipment is cut back, and the economy moves into a downturn. In the slump, unemployment rises, and wages are driven down, thus restoring profitability and leading to a revival of investment.

An enormous and largely impenetrable literature exists on whether Marx believed – and if he did so, whether it is true – that this process of cycles is set against a long-run tendency for the rate of profit to fall, which means the process of capitalism is ultimately doomed. Like Odin's doomed legions of the slain in Valhalla, capitalists in this view of the world do daily battle to protect profitability, only to fall for ever at the time of Götterdämmerung. But given that capitalism is still thriving over a century after Marx wrote, this debate seems rather irrelevant.

Marx remains one of the few economists to have articulated an endogenous theory of business cycles. As we saw in Chapter 5, during the second half of the nineteenth century an entirely different way of thinking came to dominate economic theory. In its natural state, the economy would be in equilibrium, in a state of rest. The price mechanism was posited as the means by which any disturbances to the system would be dampened, and equilibrium restored. According to this way of thinking, the economy could not possibly contain within itself any tendencies which would lead it to be in a constant state of change.

These ideas have so permeated economics that very few attempts have been made to follow in the tradition of the early economists and to develop theories in which the existence of cycles is an integral feature of the economy. In the 1930s Keynes was one of the few to do so, and he essentially proposed a psychological theory of the cycle, in which decisions are very strongly motivated by the expectations and what he termed the 'animal spirits' of business people.

Keynes saw investment decisions as the key determinant of aggregate economic activity. And since investment is carried out in the face of uncertainty about the future, companies can often make mistakes. In particular, they can get carried along by waves of optimism, which eventually prove unjustified. The economy proves not to be quite as buoyant as companies anticipated. Optimism then gives way to pessimism, investment is cut back, growth slows down and the economy moves into recession. At some point, businesses realize that their views were too pessimistic, and begin to increase investment once again.

Keynes's theory seems very realistic and appealing, and it is one to which we return in the next chapter. But Keynes himself never articulated it in a formal way, as he himself recognized. In his *magnum opus*, the *General Theory of Employment* published in 1936, his analysis of the cycle is confined to the final section of the book, entitled 'Short Notes

Suggested by the General Theory', and even within this it forms just one section headed 'Notes on the Trade Cycle'.

In a different vein, the Cambridge academic Richard Goodwin proposed a particularly interesting and elegant extension of the basic idea of Ricardo and Marx on the source of business cycles in the 1960s. Goodwin drew on ideas from mathematical biology to locate the source of cycles very firmly in the labour market. The insights into economic and social behaviour provided by the ants model were not available to him at the time, but Goodwin, along with Keynes, has been an inspirational figure to economists working outside the orthodox tradition, not least for his fundamental insight that we should be looking to the world of biology and not that of engineering if we are ever to understand the economy better.*

A widespread phenomenon in biology is 'prey-predator' systems. A classic example is the relationship between lynx and hares in the Canadian Arctic, for which a much-studied series of data exists. The lynx and the hares have absolutely irreconcilable interests, for the lynx only survive by eating the hares. Yet the two populations survive in a symbiotic relationship which is beneficial to both. If the lynx catch too many hares and drive them into extinction, they themselves will starve. But if the hares prove particularly elusive and evade capture so that the lynx die out, over-population will lead to their own food source, moss, being depleted. Eventually, the hares, too, will die.

This relationship can be stated in technical terms as a pair of non-linear differential equations known as a Volterra system, after Vito Volterra, who first proposed the idea in relationship to fish populations in the Atlantic in the 1920s in his book *A Mathematical Theory of the Struggle for Life*. A key feature of such systems is that their solutions generate permanent cycles in the populations of their component species. Suppose the lynx have a successful period of catching and devouring hares, so the population of the latter falls. The lynx will initially prosper, but then begin to die out through lack of their source of food. This gives the hares the chance to revive and to build up their population again. The rising number of hares gives more opportunities to the deprived lynx, whose

---

* Richard Goodwin died in 1997, and a formal appreciation of his theoretical work is given in my article with Mehgnad Desai in the *Economic Journal* in 1998.

numbers then increase, thereby depleting the hares once more, and so on for ever.

In Goodwin's model, there are two antagonistic classes, workers and capitalists. Contrary to what a true Marxist believer might expect, it is the workers and not the capitalists who play the role of the aggressive predator. Through their wage demands, they prey upon the share of profits in national income. Apart from this subtle reversal of roles from the Marxist view of the exploitative capitalist, the mechanics of the economic cycle follow the lines discussed by Marx. But in terms of being able to account for the short-term business cycle, the Goodwin model has a major weakness, which can be stated quite simply. The cycles which it generates are far too regular to be at all consistent with the empirical evidence. As an approach it has many strengths, and it gives a good account of a number of the key empirical phenomena observed in the Western market economies. But the regularity of its cycles constitutes a serious failing.* As we have seen, the duration and size of actual economic cycles vary widely, unlike the solutions of the Goodwin model.

But the principal line of attack by the economic mainstream against theories of the business cycle such as those of Keynes and Goodwin has nothing to do with the empirical evidence either for or against them. It is, in a sinister and damning phrase within economics, that they lack micro-foundations.

Much of what Keynes wrote, and almost all the vast subsequent literature on Keynesianism, describes behaviour at the aggregate level of the economy. In other words, the cyclical theories advanced by economists working outside the conventional view are theories about how the economy behaves overall. The relationships in these models are not derived rigorously from a theory about how economic agents – individuals and firms, in everyday English – make decisions. They purport to describe the aggregate consequences of such decisions, but do not tell us how they were arrived at by individual agents.

The central core of conventional theory is a view about how the individual behaves, about how he or she maximizes utility in a rational way, given all the information which is available. As we have seen, an

---

* This underlying regularity persists even when the equations of the model are clothed in substantial amounts of dynamic noise.

essential part of this intellectual framework is that the properties of the system as a whole can be derived simply by summing the behaviour of its component parts. Macro-economics, the theory of how the economy operates at the aggregate level, should be built on the same theoretical foundations as micro-economics.

Currently the most fashionable manifestation of the conventional approach is the 'real business cycle' theory, or RBC for short. RBC theory now dominates large sections of the academic economic community. The best journals in the United States, such as the *American Economic Review*, do carry articles that are highly critical of the approach. But elsewhere, RBC theory is the very height of fashion, with Britain's leading journal, the *Economic Journal*, devoting a large part of one of its recent issues to the concept.

RBC theory warrants extensive discussion. Despite its many weaknesses – which appear to be ultimately fatal to the theory – it has been responsible for a number of innovations. As we shall soon see, RBC theorists have placed a new – within economics at least – and wholly welcome emphasis on the need to test theories empirically. And, importantly, the particular approach to testing which they have pioneered offers a way round the quagmire of conventional methods of quantitative model-building in economics as described in the previous chapter.

Not the least of the attractions of RBC theory to conventional economists is that it does offer an explanation of the business cycle that is firmly within the orthodox tradition. A detailed mathematical description of such a model would cause most people to recoil in horror; those with strong nerves might care to glance at Appendix 2, and then hurry back to this chapter.

But the approach can be described quite straightforwardly. At any point in time, individual agents have complete knowledge of how the economy behaves, and have access to all the relevant information. Their own tastes are fixed. When in work, an individual earns money, which can be spent or saved; and savings can be used to finance periods of leisure when a person may choose to work less or not at all. Given their preferences, individuals use their understanding of the economy to decide the mixture over time of work and leisure which will maximize their own utility.

The vital assumption of RBC models is that there is an endless sequence of random shocks quite external to the economy itself. Technological innovations are usually invoked as being a plausible economic source of these necessary random shocks.* A positive shock means that the economy has the potential, for a period, to grow faster than usual – so individuals will have a stronger than average incentive in such a period to work rather than stay at home, because they can earn money more rapidly. In contrast, when a negative shock occurs, the incentive to choose leisure rather than work increases. People will accordingly adjust the number of hours they choose to work over time. These adjustments form a key part of the business cycle. When, on average, individuals choose to work less, economic growth is slow, and when they choose to work more it is fast.

The RBC approach may seem wholly unrealistic, but this is not in itself a sufficient reason to reject the theory. Any theory must necessarily abstract from and be a drastic simplification of reality. The test of a theory is whether or not it offers a satisfactory account of the phenomenon it is trying to explain.

Mark Twain once commented on Wagner's music. 'It is not', he said, 'as bad as it sounds.' The same might be said of RBC models. For their accounts of the business cycle – something which is observed at the aggregate level – are based firmly on the behaviour of individuals. The idea that the behaviour of a system as a whole should be derived from the actions of its individual components has a powerful logic to it. Indeed, a key aspect of our ants model follows this principle exactly. The colony as a whole visits the two food sites in proportions which vary over time. But this phenomenon is not the direct focus of attention in the model. Rather, the model consists of rules of behaviour which the *individual* ants follow. And from these rules the outcome for the colony *as a whole* is accounted for.

So, perhaps rather paradoxically, in this important respect the reasoning of conventional economics fits in with the general themes of this book. Behaviour at the aggregate, macro level must be explained by

---

* Technology is the most prevalent but by no means the only potential source of shocks to the economy that has been proposed as the cause of cyclical behaviour in the RBC models. A long list pervades the literature, including factors such as money and credit, the foreign sector and more abstruse concepts.

the behaviour of the individual agents at the micro level. There is, of course, a profound difference between the world of RBC theory and that of our ants. In the former, the behaviour of the system as a whole is simply the sum of its individual component parts, and can be understood by examining the behaviour of a single, representative individual. With our ants, the direct interactions between individuals make this impossible. The rules that individuals follow may be simple, but the system as a whole is complex.

A further attraction of the RBC approach is that its protagonists have, from the outset, confronted their theoretical models with empirical evidence. This has been an entirely welcome development in American economics in recent years. For decades, theory and evidence in economics rarely if ever made contact with each other. Even now there are respectable journals crammed with theoretical articles written almost entirely in calculus which may or may not have any bearing on reality. But increasingly, theorists are being compelled to look at the evidence.

A general evaluation of the performance of RBC models against actual data raises a number of subtle and important concepts. In Chapter 7 we documented the failure of conventional statistical modelling to make any progress in understanding how economies operate, despite several decades of intensive research. The methodology put forward by RBC theorists not only offers a way of testing models that avoids this problem, but is also more genuinely scientific. This is probably the most important advance made by the RBC approach.

Many readers may at this stage sympathize instinctively with the novelist Len Deighton, who once said he was not interested in the details of any argument. He just wanted to know who gets hanged at the end of it. For those who want a short cut, at the end of the chapter it is the RBC models which are swinging from the gallows. Despite the apparent sophistication of their approach, they completely fail to capture the key characteristics of the post-war business cycle in the United States, by far the largest and most important economy in the world.

Attempts have been made, within the framework of RBC theory, to estimate how much of the fluctuations in post-war American output is due to technology shocks. A figure of around 70 per cent has become the conventional wisdom. But Martin Eichenbaum, of Northwestern

University and the Federal Reserve Bank of Chicago, has recently demonstrated the enormous uncertainty which surrounds this calculation. Writing in the *Economic Journal* in 1995, Eichenbaum concluded that 'the percentage of aggregate fluctuations that technology shocks actually account for could be 70 per cent, but it could also be 5 per cent or even 200 per cent. Under these circumstances, it seems awfully hard to attach any importance to the . . . estimates pervading the literature.'

Figure 8.2 plots the quarterly growth rate of output in America over the post-war period over time – the same data which was plotted in three-dimensional form in Figure 6.7 – with the solid horizontal line showing its average value of just under 1 per cent.

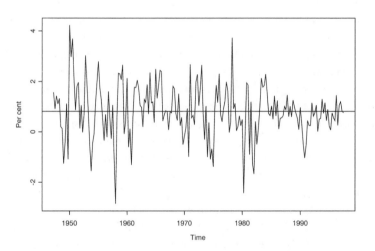

FIGURE 8.2 Quarterly rate of growth of real US GNP 1947–97

One way of trying to test the validity of the RBC approach would be to obtain a single solution of a model such as that set out in Appendix 2, and see how closely the data which emerged corresponded to the actual data. In other words, the equations could be solved to produce a series of hypothetical output growth over the same number of observations as there are in the genuine data. In the jargon, such a series is referred to as the 'simulated' data, and this is the term which will now be used to describe data series generated by solving theoretical models.

The simulated data could be plotted, and overlaid on the real data in Figure 8.2 to see how closely the simulated series followed the path of the actual, how well it mimicked the various ups and downs which have occurred. In essence, this is what number-crunching econometricians are trying to do when they build the kinds of large-scale models of the economy discussed in Chapter 7.

The process of making a proper comparison between the simulated data and the actual in this way involves a number of sophisticated statistical nuances which need not concern us here. Essentially, the basic idea is simple: plot the actual data over time; plot the simulated data on a transparency, lay it over that of the real thing, and see how closely they correspond.*

But, in this case, this procedure simply will not do. The essence of real business cycle models is that cycles exist only because of a series of random shocks administered to the economy. So a single solution to an RBC model will produce a simulated series of output growth which depends upon the particular sequence of shocks. Since these are random, the result might not give a good account at any point in time of the actual data. In other words, any single solution of an RBC model depends in part upon the particular sequence of random numbers which are used as the external shocks to the model itself. In contrast, in real life there is only one 'solution', namely the actual data on the American economy.

An important clue as to how to go about comparing the solutions of RBC models with real data is given by what might at first sight appear to be a brief digression into aspects of probability. Suppose we are asked to test whether a coin is a fair one or not. Perhaps some hapless friend has lost a large amount of money in a long game of guessing the outcome of the toss of the coin, and wants to see if he has been duped. We might send the coin for laboratory analysis, to have it measured for physical bias, but the simplest thing to do is to sit down and toss the coin ourselves a thousand times, say, and to note down the outcomes. We can then do

* More precisely, to avoid the wrath of econometricians, they focus their attention principally on the differences between the actual and the simulated data, and carry out a wide range of statistical tests on these differences.

exactly the same thing with a coin which we think is fair, such as one just drawn out of a bank.*

In this experiment, the outcome of the series of tosses with the coin fresh from the bank is contrasted with that of the coin used in the gambling game. The greater the discrepancy between the two, the more likely it is that the two coins are not the same: one is fair and the other is not.

The same principles can be used to compare the simulated output growth of a real business cycle model with actual data. By solving a real business cycle model a large number of times, the irregularities which exist in any individual solution will be ironed out when the results are averaged. The greater the discrepancy between the properties of the actual data and of the average of the simulated data, the more reasonable it is for us to decide that the theoretical model does not give a good description of reality.

The trick is to decide what are the important distinguishing features of the actual data with which to compare the average of the outcome of the simulations. In terms of our ants model, for example, the key fact to be explained was that the proportion of the colony visiting any one of the food sites was in a constant state of change. The biologists who set up the experiments had thought up a sophisticated theory about what would happen to this proportion over time. This required, as explained in the opening chapter, that the proportion would settle at a fixed amount, after a certain amount of initial fluctuations. The amount itself could be anything between zero and one hundred per cent, a key part of the theory being that this could not be predicted in advance. This latter point proved true in the experiments, but, in direct contradiction to their theory, the proportion never settled to a fixed amount. The more general theory put forward by Alan Kirman accounts for this key fact, as well as being consistent with the other aspects of behaviour of the colony explained by the biologists' theory.

Real business cycle theorists themselves have focused on two particular aspects. First, the variability of the output data. In other words, the

---

* Of course, in this example, we could use probability theory to tell us the precise chance of obtaining any given split between heads and tails on the assumption that the coin is a fair one.

typical range of the rates of growth of output between the trough of a recession and the peak of the boom. Second, the variability of the different components of output relative to one another. RBC models typically subdivide overall output into its large component parts, such as total personal consumption and total investment. And it is the relative size of the ranges of these component parts which is of interest, as well as that of the overall output of the economy when these bits are added together.

On these criteria, RBC models do well. But it is almost trivially easy to obtain such results, certainly for the aggregate output series. More importantly, this particular choice of qualities of the data against which the simulated model data can be checked is somewhat bizarre. Its eccentricity is not so much the measure itself, but the fact that it does not focus at all on what economists usually look at when examining data series over time.

Confronted by a series of data over time, such as the quarterly growth of American GNP over the post-war period, the first thing which a statistician or econometrician would normally do is to investigate whether there is any connection between successive observations.* For example, if the output growth is high in any particular period, can anything be said about the growth rate which will typically follow in the next period? Will it, too, be high, or low, or is there an equal chance of it being either?

The formal calculation of this gives a measure known as the correlation between growth in any given period and in the period immediately before it. This concept is important, for it gives an indication as to the essential structure of the data over time. The correlation can take values between +1 and -1, with +1 meaning a perfect positive correlation, and -1 a perfect negative one. In other words, a value close to +1 shows that high output growth now is very likely to be followed by high growth in the next period, while one of close to -1 indicates that the series is likely to go to the other extreme of a recession. And a correlation of close to zero shows that there is no connection between values now and values in the next period: no matter where we start from, there is not a great deal that can usefully be said about what is likely to happen in the next period.

---

* Actually, the very first thing one should do is to plot the data and inspect it, a task often neglected by younger econometricians. The combination of the human eye and brain can be a very powerful one.

Correlations are usually calculated not just between the data in any given period and the one immediately before or after it, but between observations which are separated by several periods. Given that the actual data is quarterly output growth and that there are four quarters in a year, economists naturally look at correlations between growth now and growth two, three and four periods ago, and perhaps even extend the comparison to cover a couple of years, or eight periods. The term which is used to describe the successive individual correlations between data in any given period and data one, two, three or more periods ago is the auto-correlation function, or ACF.

Post-war American output growth data has a very clear pattern in its ACF. While none of the individual correlations which make up the ACF are strong, the qualitative picture is well defined. The correlations between growth in any given period and growth both in the period immediately before and in the one before that, are low but positive. In other words, a high or a low growth rate in any particular period tends to be followed by a high or low one both in the next period and in the one after that. The connection is not very powerful, because the correlations are not strong (being around 0.40 and 0.25 respectively). But, on balance, high or low growth in any given quarter is more likely than not to be followed for the next two quarters by high or low growth.

Beyond these very short-run correlations, the pattern is much weaker. The correlation between growth now and growth in nine or twelve months' time, three and four quarters ahead respectively, is very close to, but just below, zero. The relationship between growth in any particular quarter and growth in any of the quarters one to two years ahead is effectively zero but, if anything, slightly below it.

During the mid-1990s, economists such as Martin Eichenbaum, Timothy Cogley, James Nason, Julio Rotemberg and Michael Woodford looked at the sort of correlations between successive periods of output growth which real business cycle models produce. They look nothing like those of actual American data. Some variants of these models give auto-correlation functions which are completely negative, and others give ones which are zero throughout. The actual data, in contrast, has an ACF which starts off distinctly positive, becomes negative, and then wobbles about on or just below the zero line.

From any remotely serious scientific standpoint, real business cycle models fail to account for a fundamental property of the post-war business cycle in the United States. The obsession with the variability of the data has led real business cycle theorists to miss what Martin Eichenbaum has called 'first order failure' of their models.

A second principle has been introduced into the testing procedure. The auto-correlation function is the standard and straightforward way of describing a data series in what is called the time domain. In other words, it looks for basic structure in the data over time. A different perspective, which is widely used in disciplines such as electrical engineering, examines what is known as the frequency domain.* The essential idea is to examine the fluctuations in a series of data plotted over time, such as the American output growth data in Figure 8.2, and to see how these can be broken down into a number of separate, component series, each of which has *completely regular* movements over time.

We came across the basic principles of this idea in the discussion of our three-dimensional charts in Chapter 6. An important feature of the mathematical techniques which are used is that they can rank the individual, regular cycles which are discovered in order of their importance in making up the data being examined.

When these techniques are applied to US data, the most important regular component cycles are those whose duration corresponds to what is usually thought of as being the period of the business cycle. There are a variety of whistles and bells which can be used with these techniques, and the results can vary slightly depending upon which ones we blow or ring. But the main component cycles of US output data are those which have a duration of between two and seven years. While these are not enormously stronger than cycles of shorter or longer duration, analysis nevertheless gives a consistent picture that cycles of these durations are more powerful than the rest. In other words, the duration of the business cycle is typically between two and seven years.

In contrast, real business cycle models give simulated output growth series which bear no resemblance to this at all. In fact, it is very hard to

---

* Of course, given that the power spectrum is the Fourier transform pair of the auto-correlation function, there is a direct connection between the two. But an exposition of this point is a matter for textbooks in mathematics and not this book.

distinguish a component cycle of such data which is any more powerful than any of the others. Cycles of, say, three months' duration, are just as important as those of four years, or even those of ten years.

So, on two standard methods of investigation, in the time and frequency domains, solutions of real business cycle models do not match the properties of the actual post-war American business cycle data. These are very serious failures. The continued grip of these models on the academic economic community is yet another illustration of Mark Twain's remark that the difference between fact and fiction is that fiction has to be plausible.

But, in the broader context, RBC theorists have performed a service by advancing within conventional economics the need to confront even the most abstract theory with actual data. And they have offered a way forward to more effective testing of a wide range of models.

A number of leading American economists are scathing about RBC models, not merely on the grounds of their empirical failures. Joseph Stiglitz, former chairman of the Council of Economic Advisers, gave the Marshall Lectures at Cambridge University in 1996. He opened in superb fashion. 'Real business cycle theory,' he began, picking up the first sheet of his notes and casting it to the ground, 'that's about all that needs to be said about that.' Paul Krugman is also caustic, quoting approvingly a comment that 'RBC theory is becoming like a fringe political movement that successively purges itself of the ideologically impure until only a handful of members are left'. He has given an amusing but nevertheless very serious reason for the fascination of the economics profession with a theory which he regards as being wholly misguided. In *Peddling Prosperity* he writes, 'the technicality and difficulty of [contemporary and conventional economic] theory is, in the world of academic economics, an asset rather than a liability. It is cynical but true to say that in the academic world the theories that are most likely to attract a devoted following are those that best allow a clever but not very original young man to demonstrate his cleverness.'

But there is a further twist to RBC theory which attracts the particular ridicule of serious scholars such as Krugman and Stiglitz. The actual fluctuations which we observe in output are considerably greater than those which are seen in the average output produced per hour by each worker. The difference is made up by the relatively large fluctuations in the number of hours worked. RBC theorists account for this by assuming that people *choose* to work fewer hours following an adverse technology shock. These individuals operate rationally, and behave in a way which maximizes their utility over the course of a lifetime. Following a positive technology shock, productivity will be high, so people decide to work longer hours. But when a negative one occurs and productivity is temporarily low, people choose, rationally, to take leisure time rather than to work. In other words, in Krugman's words, according to this theory we could see the Great Depression of the 1930s as an 'extended voluntary holiday'.

Even many economists who are sympathetic to the real business cycle approach feel the occasional doubt about the realism of its fundamental assumptions. In many ways, they are in the position of Mr Prendergast, the prison chaplain in Evelyn Waugh's *Decline and Fall*. Provided he were able to overcome his doubt as to why God had made the world at all, he could see that 'everything else follows – Tower of Babel, Babylonian captivity, Incarnation, Church, bishops, incense, everything'.

Mike Wickens, one of the editors of the *Economic Journal*, made a comment in that journal's recent symposium on RBC theory with which many would agree: 'For many the appeal of Keynesian economics over [orthodox] economics is the supposed greater realism of its assumptions. We all know that markets are not complete, that people are not rational, make myopic decisions and lack full information, that one agent is different from another, and that a model built on micro-economic foundations cannot be aggregated to the level of conventional macro-economic variables. The problem is that building models with these features is virtually an intractable problem.'

The challenge of building such a model is one to which we now turn.

CHAPTER 9

Through a Glass Darkly

Our flexible friends the ants have already helped to illuminate a wide range of economic and social questions. The basic principles of their behaviour, suitably adapted to the particular circumstances, are able to give good accounts of what happens in the real world. From Hollywood to the foreign exchange markets, from the pattern of crime rates to why economic forecasts fail, the idea that individuals can be influenced directly by the behaviour of others is a powerful one.

An explanation of the business cycle, one of *the* most important phenomena of the Western economies, can also be provided by the concepts which underpin our model of ant behaviour.

In the previous chapter, we noted extensive parallels between key features of actual business cycles and the behaviour of the colony in the simple ants model. For example, the rate of growth of the economy as a whole is in a constant state of change, and never settles down at some fixed point. Exactly the same is observed with the proportion of the ant colony visiting any particular site. Both the economy and the behaviour of the ant colony are very difficult to predict in the short term. And the periodicity of the business cycle is irregular, as are the fluctuations in the proportion of ants at one of the food sources.

There are differences as well as similarities. For example, with the economy, although the time period of its various booms and recessions is irregular, it is not completely without a pattern. There is evidence of a cycle of somewhere between two and seven years and, as we saw in the previous chapter, building a model which captures this subtle aspect of behaviour is very challenging.

But there are other ways in which business cycles and the ant colony correspond in terms of behaviour. Although the movements of the colony cannot be predicted in the short term, in the longer term a very distinctive pattern is observed. Recall Figures 1.2 and 1.3, which show the relative amounts of time different proportions of the colony spend visiting a particular site. We can never say at any particular time exactly what the proportion will be, but we can say how much of the time a particular proportion will be observed. The same sort of structure seems to exist in business cycle data. Figure 8.2 in the previous chapter shows the quarterly rate of growth of the post-war American economy over time. Figure 9.1 takes exactly the same data and presents it in a different way. This figure shows the number of times the rate of growth has been within different bands.

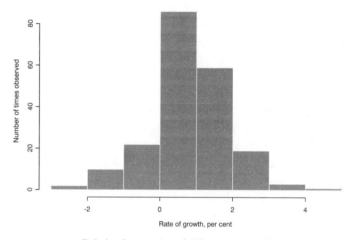

FIGURE 9.1 Relative frequencies of different economic growth rates, US economy 1947–97

Reading across from the top of the highest bar to the left-hand axis, we can see that growth was in the range 0–1 per cent in some eighty quarterly periods between 1947 and 1997. The next most frequently observed range was between 1 and 2 per cent. Far less frequently, and in an approximately equal number of quarters, there was either a mild recession, with growth between 0 and -1 per cent, or a rapid expansion when growth was between 2 and 3 per cent. At the extremes, we can see there have been occasions when growth fell below -1 per cent, in deep recessions, and times when it was exceptionally strong at over 3 per cent. But these are few and far between.

Figure 9.1 shows that, over time, the short-term growth of the American economy does have a distinctive pattern. Although we can effectively never say which of the bands any particular quarter in the future will be in,* we can say very sensible things about how frequently we expect any particular rate of growth to be observed. Much of the time, growth will be mildly positive, but every so often there will be a sharp recession and, just as infrequently, a dramatic up-turn. In the same way, with our ants we have a very good idea of how often any given split of the colony between the two food sites will be observed.

So, the basic ants model generates results for the colony as a whole which have many parallels with observations of the world's largest economy over the course of its business cycles. But, as in most of our examples, the ants have to be modified to deal with specific problems. In the case of the business cycle, we need to give an economic account of the behaviour of the individual agents, who are the equivalent of the ants in our model.

An important theoretical point about the model is that it is inhabited by individual actors, the ants. It is their reactions to each other's behaviour which produces the fluctuations in the proportions of the colony visiting a food site. So these oscillations and changes in *aggregate* behaviour follow directly from the complex ways in which individual agents act.

In short, the ants model does have very clear micro-foundations. So, too, does our model of the business cycle. It is based very firmly on individual agents acting according to particular rules, which involve changing behaviour as a direct result of observing the behaviour of others – the behaviour of individuals gives rise to the patterns which are observed at the aggregate level, in terms of the economy as a whole.

In our model of the business cycle, the actors empathize with T. S. Eliot's phrase, 'My people, humble people'. They have no great pretence to know the future, indeed they are content to form views no further ahead than a single period of time. They do not carry out complicated mathematical manipulations to guide their decisions, and, far from expecting to be proved right, are pleasantly surprised when they are. For

* There is, as noted in Chapter 6, a very mild degree of predictability of US data, but it is not strong.

the future, even one period ahead, is shrouded in uncertainty, in what Keynes described as 'the dark forces of time and ignorance'.

The agents act according to some very simple rules. Each agent is slightly different – they inhabit a diverse cosmos, in which no two agents are exactly alike – but every one of them sets great store by what other people think, and allows his or her decisions to be influenced by opinion in general.*

In the economic sense of the term, the agents in our model are distinctly non-rational. They follow simple rules of thumb as a good guide to reasonable decision-making in a complex and uncertain world.

In so far as the approach can be located within the traditions of economic theory, the behaviour of the individual agents can be thought of as being broadly consistent with the economics of Keynes. Expectations about what other people think and uncertainty about the future are crucial elements in the model. And, as we noted in the previous chapter, Keynes's theory of the business cycle was largely based on these psychological elements. An important difference in our approach, of course, is that the maths and the technology are now available to formalize these factors into explicit rules of behaviour, and to give micro-foundations to a non-orthodox theory of the business cycle.

An implication of this pedigree of our model is that the business cycle exists because of qualities which are inherent within the economic system itself. In the jargon, it is endogenous. There is no need to invoke an endless series of random shocks external to the economy to account for the existence of the business cycle. This is not to say that such shocks never happen in practice. But they are not necessary in our model to produce an endless series of short-term fluctuations in overall output.

Companies are the bedrock of capitalist economies. They create wealth, generate product innovations, and make decisions on wages and employment levels which affect the prosperity of individuals throughout the economy. Accordingly, our model focuses on the behaviour of firms, rather than on that of private individuals. Companies play the role of ants. Of course, this is just one way in which the theoretical model represents a

---

* The model described below is summarized in mathematical format, for those so inclined, in Appendix 3.

dramatic abstraction of reality. The same is true for any model, for any map, and what counts is whether, despite its enormous simplifications, it is able to give a reasonable description of the world it purports to portray.

For Western economies, data on national output is available on a quarterly basis. For some economies, tentative estimates are made on a monthly basis, but the period of three months is the one for which data is normally published. So, to enable direct comparisons to be made with actual data, actions within our model take place on a quarter by quarter basis.

A key question which every firm must decide during any particular quarter is the rate of growth of the output which it will produce in the next quarter. Once this decision has been made, the firm is stuck with it. In due course the company arrives in this next quarter and it is then allowed to decide a different growth rate for the following quarter, but not to revise the previous decision on this quarter's growth. Obviously, this is a somewhat artificial assumption, but it is not completely unreasonable. For, in the very short run, there are often substantial costs involved in altering previous decisions about how much to produce. Contracts have been placed with suppliers, the workforce has been alerted as to how much effort will be needed – indeed employees may have been either taken on or sacked depending upon the circumstances – the marketing programme will be committed, and so on.

In these circumstances, our firms need a straightforward rule in order to decide how quickly output should be expanded or contracted in the next period. They are very short-sighted, and look no further ahead than this, operating on the Biblical precept of 'sufficient unto the day is the evil thereof'. Despite their myopia and apparent simplicity, they are quite shrewd in understanding that a simple rule for decision-making may serve them rather well, and allow them to reach satisfactory decisions a fair amount of the time. In Herbert Simon's phrase, they 'satisfice' rather than 'maximize'. Certainly, they do not need to hire theoretical economists who will solve complicated problems of inter-temporal maximization for them, and they save on fees by eschewing the services of management consultants.

One factor which weighs in a company's decision on how much to alter the amount produced in the next period is the rate of growth at which output is actually changing during the current period. We have already noted the costs which might be incurred if previous decisions are changed too quickly, and there are difficulties in altering the amount which a firm is producing by large amounts, whether up or down. So a certain amount of inertia is built into the system.

But far more importantly, in deciding the rate at which its own output is to change in the next period, each firm pays great attention to the general feeling – the degree of optimism or pessimism – about the future, and how this is changing.

There are sound reasons for behaving like this. If, for example, general expectations about the future are rather depressed, it is sensible to take this into account when deciding how much one's own production should change in the next period. The risks of trying to buck the trend, of gearing up for a substantial expansion, are considerable. At the other extreme, if there is general optimism about the future, a decision not to increase output could well lead to a loss of potential sales and hence of profits.

Keynes set great store on the role of expectations and the general level of confidence in determining the outcome of the economy, both in the short run and, through decisions on investment, in the longer term. He also emphasized the importance for an individual firm of paying close attention to the general level of sentiment when taking decisions. In part, he thought this was necessary as a cynical defence of one's own position. 'Worldly wisdom', he wrote, 'teaches that it is far better for reputation to fail conventionally than to succeed unconventionally.' In other words, a chief executive or chairman who did rather badly for the company would emerge in a better light if he or she had followed the prevailing wisdom than if apparently rash decisions had been taken. Equally, however, Keynes believed that there were positive reasons for acting in this way. If everyone else is thought to base their actions to a large extent on the general level of sentiment about the future, a strategy of not doing so runs very considerable risks. 'Entrepreneurs will find it financially advantageous, and often unavoidable, to fall in with the ideas of the market, even though they themselves are better instructed.'

Our model, then, is very Keynesian in spirit. But quite a few more bricks need to be put in place before the edifice is complete. One question, for example, is how individual firms discover what the general sentiment about the future is at any given point. There is a simple practical answer to this. Information is widely available in the financial press. Company reports, interim statements by chairmen about company prospects, the views of market analysts anticipating outcomes on sales and profits – all these and much more are available at an extremely reasonable price by purchasing a newspaper such as the *Wall Street Journal* or the *Financial Times.** In this way, a picture can be readily built up about the level of business sentiment about the future and about how it is changing.

Agents in our model form a view about the general level of optimism or pessimism about the future amongst firms as a whole. In technical terms, the interaction between agents takes place at the aggregate, or global, level. The behaviour of each company is influenced by the sentiment of the group of firms as a whole. This is in contrast with the basic ants model, where each individual ant can only interact with the small number of other ants it encounters as it leaves the nest.

But an essential ingredient of the model is still missing. The general level of business optimism or pessimism about the future is inescapably linked with uncertainty. After all, it might not prove to be accurate. Expectations might be buoyant, for example, but if enough companies at any one time shade them down in their own calculations and decisions, the actual growth of output in the next period will be rather modest.

This leads directly to the really crucial element in our model. The inherent uncertainty about anything connected with the future leads each of the individual companies in our model to interpret a given level of overall sentiment about the future *in a slightly different way*.

Individual circumstances and attitudes to risk differ. So a firm which has had an aggressive policy of expansion might choose to consolidate its gains rather than ride its luck too far when business sentiment becomes more optimistic, whereas another firm in similar circumstances might become even more assertive and plan to grow even faster.

On a more practical plane, there may very well be uncertainty about the exact level of overall business sentiment at any point. Although business

---

* These newspapers even report, for what they are worth, forecasts for the economy as a whole, so they can be obtained for a few cents or pence a day instead of the more exotic fees the forecasters themselves charge for their work.

surveys do exist, they are just one more piece of information which goes to make up the overall picture. Firms can get a pretty good idea from the financial press about how other people's views are changing, but it will never be definitive.

In short, uncertainty means that each firm operates in a different way from every other firm. There is uncertainty at any point in time about the precise level of business sentiment about the future. And there is uncertainty about what any perceived level of sentiment means for any particular firm when deciding how much its output should grow in the period immediately ahead. Firms are different; in the jargon of economics, our agents are heterogenous. We do not require that any particular firm be consistently more optimistic or pessimistic than any other. All that is needed is the assumption that at each point in time each firm assesses the consequences of uncertainty differently.

Within the confines of our model, we can now pull together the two factors which determine how firms decide on the rate of growth of output in the period immediately ahead. In part, this is governed by inertia, by how much they have increased or cut back production during the present period. But they also take account of, and in fact give much more weight to, the general level of business sentiment about the future, and how this is changing. This is all that is needed for one half of our model.

To complete the system, we need a rule for deciding how sentiment about the future is formed. One element, again, is the presence of inertia. It is tiresome and costly to go through the process of revising views about the future, so the degree of optimism or pessimism which any firm holds about the future in the current period will partly depend upon what it thought in the previous period.

We have already specified how the rate of output in the model is determined. In the interests of seeing how far we can get with the simplest possible model, we try to form a link between output growth and sentiment. An important clue is provided once again by Keynes, who defined the trade cycle, as he called the business cycle, in the following way: 'By a cyclical movement we mean that as the system progresses in, e.g., the upward direction, the forces propelling it upwards at first gather force and have a cumulative effect on one another but gradually lose their strength until at a certain point they tend to be replaced by forces operating in the opposite direction; which in turn gather force for a time and accentuate one another, until they too, having reached their maximum development, wane and give rise to the opposite.'

Keynes was originally trained as a mathematician, and he could easily have condensed this elegant and involved sentence into a single line in a very simple equation. For what he is describing is the theoretical ideal of an oscillator, or pendulum. At one of the extremes of its swing, the pendulum is virtually stationary. As it moves back towards the middle of its arc, it gathers speed and then gradually slows as it progresses to the other extreme of its range. Translated into a mathematical formula, this implies that the rate of change of the rate of change depends negatively on the position of the pendulum. The key here is the negative connection: the further away from the centre of its arc, the stronger the acceleration towards the centre.

This is the principle which we introduce into the expression determining how the sentiment about the future of each individual firm changes. We postulate that the firm looks at the rate of growth of overall output in the current period. If it is high, then, other things being equal, the firm is likely to become somewhat more pessimistic, while if it is low, the firm starts to take a more optimistic view of the future. In other words, there is a negative relationship between the actual overall growth of output, and the change in sentiment about the future of any individual firm. If the economy is in a boom, for example, firms start to think that it cannot last.

And, once again, the important principle of uncertainty is introduced, so each firm interprets the implications of a given rate of growth of total output slightly differently.

In essence, then, we are proposing a model which is a dramatic simplification of reality. Each firm's rate of growth of output in the next period depends upon its own current rate of growth, and the rate at which overall sentiment about the future is changing, overall sentiment being simply the average of the views of all the individual firms, weighted by the size of the firm. The rate of change of sentiment about the future of any individual firm depends upon how its views about the present changed in the recent past, and on how fast overall output is growing. And each firm, because of uncertainty about the future, interprets the implications of both the aggregate sentiment and output terms slightly differently.

Despite their apparently uncomplicated nature, these two equations are fiendishly difficult to solve using pencil and paper. As with real business cycle models, we have to rely upon computer-generated results – simulations – in order to give us a sufficiently large number of solutions with which to judge the properties of the model.

The rate of growth of overall output arising from a typical solution of the model is plotted in Figure 9.2.* While remembering that we are not trying to reproduce in any way the exact path of post-war US output growth, the data here does seem to bear a qualitative resemblance to that of actual output growth, shown in the previous chapter in Figure 8.2. There are lots of erratic movements up and down, but with perhaps some discernible, more regular rhythms amongst the confusion.

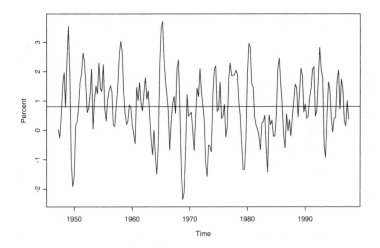

FIGURE 9.2 Output growth variable in a typical simulation

But, as with real business cycle models, the true test lies in a comparison with the underlying structure of the real data. We carry out a large number – a thousand – simulations of our model in order to iron out

---

* Technically, we compare the actual and simulated data net of the mean, but in the charts the data is plotted with the mean included. It does not alter in any way the conclusions.

any irregularities which might appear in a small number, and compare the key properties with those of the actual data.

The two major failings of real business cycle models identified in the literature and discussed in the previous chapter are as follows. First, they are unable to generate correlations between rates of growth in any given period and those of previous periods which remotely resemble those of actual data. Second, the data produced by RBC models does not have any cyclical structure at all.

The pattern of correlations between successive quarters in the actual American growth data – between growth in the current period and growth one, two, three and more periods ago – has a distinctive shape. As discussed in the previous chapter, the correlation between growth now and growth both one and two periods ago is positive. The relationship with data three and four periods ago is not strong, but tends to be negative. And for longer intervals, it is around zero, perhaps ever so slightly negative.

The simulated data produced by our model has exactly this property. The precise estimates of each individual correlation are not exactly the same as that of the actual data, but the qualitative pattern is identical.* (For example, the sum of the first two correlations is 0.62 in the actual data and averages 0.72 in the simulations, and the sum of the first eight is 0.27 and 0.29 respectively.)

In terms of the business cycle, too, our model produces recognizable cycles which correspond closely to the frequencies obtained when the actual data is decomposed into its regular, cyclical parts. The main components range over the two- to six- or seven-year duration, in exactly the same way as the actual data. In other words, unlike in RBC models, in our model there *is* a business cycle.

So, on the two standard tests which have been applied to test real business cycle models against actual data, our model of interacting agents, for all its apparent simplicity, performs far, far better. The results are not perfect, and there are some small differences still with the real American data. But these differences are minor compared to the dramatic empirical failure of the orthodox real business cycle approach.

---

* Interested readers can obtain a full description of the simulations via the publisher's e-mail address: sallyg@faber.co.uk.

And in the opening part of this chapter, we noted several additional ways in which the output of this kind of model paralleled that of actual business cycle data. A concrete example of this is given in Figure 9.3, which plots for a typical simulation the relative frequency of growth rates which our model generates. This can be compared directly with Figure 9.1, which plots the frequency for the actual data.

The qualitative patterns of the actual and simulated data are identical, with the most frequently observed growth range being between 0 and 1 per cent, followed by that between 1 and 2 per cent. Much less frequently, and in approximately equal numbers, we have either a mild recession with growth between 0 and -1 per cent, or a rapid expansion with growth between 2 and 3 per cent. And in each case, there is a small number of instances of more extreme observations, with deep recessions or dramatic expansions.

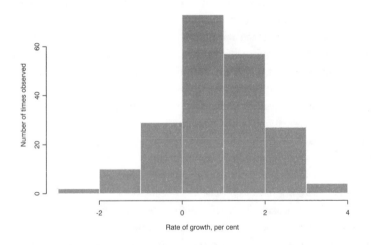

FIGURE 9.3 Relative frequency of different economic growth rates: simulated data

By this stage, the reader may start to feel sympathy with the trumpet player of a famous brass band in the North of England in the 1930s. Deeply embedded in working-class culture, such bands contended fiercely for the trophies on offer in competitions. The bandmaster in question was a martinet, who ceremoniously locked the door to the room where the band assembled in the evening to practise, permitting no one to leave until he was satisfied. The band were rehearsing Handel's *Messiah*, for the biggest competition of the year. The star trumpeter was not quite on form, and the bandmaster insisted on the same piece being played over and over again. Finally, in exasperation, he appealed to the trumpeter, 'Look, this is the most important part of the whole piece. Elijah himself appears. You've got to give it more passion. Just think what you'd feel if Elijah himself appeared before us at this very moment. What would you say?' The trumpeter thought for a moment. 'Ah'd say, Elijah, it's ten past ten, time this rehearsal were over. If tha'll come down to t' bar with me, Ah'll let thi buy me a pint.'

But, in contrast to the trumpeter, we will persevere for a bit longer. The more tests, the more criteria, which a model can satisfy when compared to reality, the more confidence we can have in it.

Thinking back to Chapter 6, we discussed non-linear signal processing, and applied it to macro-economic data series. This powerful technique can be used to understand why the actual macro-economic forecasting record has been so bad. There is simply insufficient systematic information in the data for forecasts to have any reasonable degree of accuracy over a period of time. American data, however, appears to have a certain amount of structure, a fact which the Federal Reserve in particular has been able to use to produce predictions which have had some, albeit limited, value. Forecast errors which are of a non-trivial size compared to the actual data will inevitably still be made, for the amount of useful information in the data is not large. But some structure exists.

Figure 9.4 reproduces Figure 6.7, which we used to give a feel for the results of this type of analysis when applied to post-war American output growth data. Alongside it, in Figure 9.5, is a plot of the data generated by a typical simulation of our model. Both charts reveal a substantial amount of disorder, but, not just to the fond parental eye but apparent in the underlying mathematics,* both possess a certain, similar degree of structure.

---

* This involves a comparison of the ordered eigenvalues of the covariance matrix of a delay matrix formed from the original data.

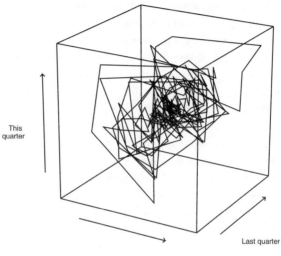

This
quarter

Last quarter

Two quarters ago

FIGURE 9.4 Three-dimensional plot of US real GDP growth

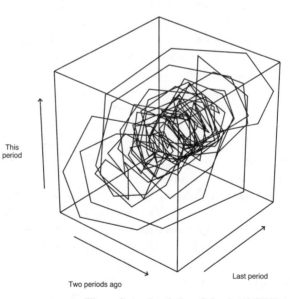

This
period

Last period

Two periods ago

FIGURE 9.5 Three-dimensional plot of simulated GDP growth

134

Yet another dimension of testing of our interacting agent model arises from its clear implication that the degree of uncertainty which exists and the amplitude, or range, of the fluctuations of the business cycle are connected. The more uncertain the climate in which our firms operate, the greater the diversity of opinion amongst them. In other words, a greater variety of interpretations will be placed by individual companies on any given change in overall output or sentiment about the future. And, in consequence, the greater is the potential for larger movements in the rate of growth of overall output, for individual firms themselves are more likely to make bigger changes in their output, whether up or down.

This prediction of the model is difficult to subject to precise testing, because readily available measures of the overall level of uncertainty do not exist. We cannot, for example, turn to the national accounts, as we can with the rate of growth of output, and read off data for uncertainty.

But we can take a longer perspective, and think about the relative degrees of uncertainty which have prevailed during different periods of economic history. Before the First World War, the global economy was very open, in many ways more so than today, with enormous capital flows. A degree of control and regulation was exercised by the Bank of England via the Gold Standard, but it was a time of massive movements of international capital, and fierce domestic struggles over the distribution of national income. In short, it was a period of considerable uncertainty.

In the inter-war years throughout the West, this intensified. A lack of certainty dominated the overall climate, even before the massive shock of the Great Depression in the 1930s. The political climate was extremely volatile, and labour militancy and unrest was at a very high level in many countries. Internationally, there were serious disagreements on the appropriate monetary order, with fierce arguments about the Gold Standard, and trade protectionism was strong.

In contrast, the first three decades after the Second World War saw a much more stable environment. Liberal democracy prevailed in almost all Western countries, and the intense political antagonisms of the inter-war years within individual countries fell away sharply. In terms of the international economic order, the monetary situation was stable, with fixed exchange rates, and barriers to trade were removed on a substantial scale.

During the 1970s, with the exception of the United States, by virtue of its size and relative economic insularity, uncertainty increased sharply. Inflation became a serious issue in many countries, in part provoked by the quadrupling of the oil price by OPEC in 1973–4, which inflicted a substantial shock on the West. The post-war monetary order broke down, and a period of fluctuating currency markets came into being. But there was no return to the international anarchy of the inter-war period, as further decisive moves were made towards international integration and the reduction of trade barriers.

The implication of our model is that the fluctuations in output over the business cycle are greater the higher is the degree of uncertainty. So we would expect that the amplitude of economic cycles would be greatest in the inter-war period, high in both the pre-First World War period and the period from the mid-1970s to the present, and lowest in the 1950s and 1960s.

Figure 9.6 plots, for a change, the annual growth of output per head in the UK since the 1870s, though again this is typical of the Western economies as a whole.

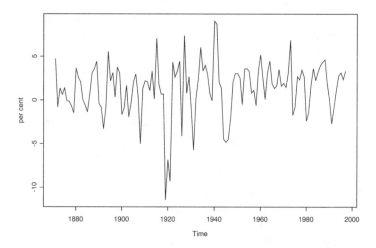

FIGURE 9.6 Rate of growth of UK real national income 1871–1997

The enormous range of movements in the inter-war period is readily apparent. A somewhat closer inspection is required to see that the variability was lowest in the 1950s and 1960s, but this is indeed the case, and can be confirmed by more formal statistical measures of the concept of variability. Looking back to the American data plotted in Figure 8.1 on p. 104, a similar story emerges, except that the variability of the US data does not increase so obviously from the 1970s onwards.

This piece of evidence in itself is by no means decisive in terms of validating our model. But it is one more piece of the jigsaw which fits. Our model predicts that higher uncertainty leads to greater fluctuations during the business cycle, and this is consistent with what we observe in reality.

In the spirit of scientific testing, we have confronted the properties and predictions of our simple model with a wide range of qualities exhibited by actual business cycle data, with the particular focus on post-war data in America, still by far the single most important economy in the world. The results are sufficiently congruent with the empirical evidence, unlike those of conventional models of the business cycle, to give a degree of confidence that the approach is reasonable. The feature of the approach which breaks most decisively with orthodoxy is the fact that the behaviour of others directly affects the behaviour of each individual agent in the model.

The policy implications of our model are somewhat paradoxical. Despite the Keynesian micro-foundations of the model – the behavioural rules followed by individual agents – the properties of the model offer little support for the concept of Keynesian 'demand management'. This is the phrase used to describe the attempts by governments to control the business cycle, which, as we saw in Chapter 6, are still widely practised throughout the West. By trying to anticipate and predict the course of the cycle, the authorities believe that adjustments to their policies – on interest rates, taxation, public spending, and so on – can smooth out the fluctuations in the economic cycle.

We saw in Chapter 6 that this was not feasible, not least because of the inherent difficulty of producing forecasts of sufficient accuracy. This is also a feature of the aggregate output growth series produced by our model, a point which follows on directly from the discussion on Figure 9.5. Although there is a small degree of underlying regularity in the short-term growth of output, the amount of structure is not high. So the ability to make short-term predictions with a reasonable degree of accuracy over time is severely limited.

Using our model simulations, a forecaster could do ever so slightly better than forecasters throughout the West have done in reality, but large errors in predictions would be unavoidable and would happen quite frequently. In practice the government would not be able to anticipate the outcome of any particular business cycle, and hence pre-empt any adverse movements by appropriate short-term interventions and policy changes.

Suppose, however, that the economy enters a period of severe depression, and the government decides to take action to offset the recession, either by spending more, or by cutting interest rates, or whatever. There is a separate and important problem as to whether governments can know what the effects of such measures will be, as we discussed in Chapter 7. But suppose for a moment that in the world of our model, the government does know.

The impact of the measures can be appreciated by looking at Figure 9.7. This plots the growth of output in a typical simulation of the model in which a *positive* external shock is applied approximately half-way through the simulation. We can think of this as being a very large stimulus applied by the government, in the form of sharp reductions in interest rates, large increases in public spending, or substantial reductions in taxation.

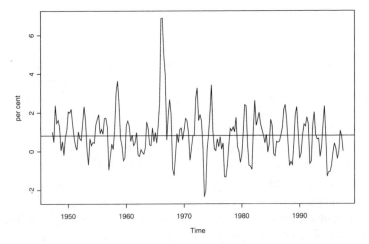

FIGURE 9.7 Growth in output with hypothetical expansionary policy

It must be emphasized that this is a purely hypothetical 'history' which arises from a typical simulation of our model. The model is started off in the late 1940s, and for around twenty years is assumed to operate of its own accord. The pattern of growth which we see over this period is similar to that in Figure 9.2, with occasional recessions and booms, but with most periods registering growth of between zero and 2 per cent.

We assume that in the late 1960s, the government decided to apply a large, temporary stimulus to the economy, equivalent to 5 per cent of output in the first year, and 2.5 per cent in the second. We can see that as a result output growth is temporarily very high at well over 6 per cent. But the impact of the stimulus eventually dies away completely and the normal pattern of growth is resumed.

So once an economy is actually in recession, the authorities can in principle move the economy out of the slump – assuming hypothetically that they know how to – by a temporary stimulus. In the longer term, however, such policies have no effect on the overall behaviour of the economy.

The strong implications of our theoretical model are that a policy stance based on the idea of anticipating and offsetting future movements in the business cycle is unlikely to be successful over time. Forecasts of sufficient accuracy cannot be made, and any temporary stimulus which is given to output by the government will have no long-term effect. The concept of short-term control is essentially illusory.

A fundamental concept in the orthodox approach is that of the multiplier – the idea that the initial impact of, say, an increase in public spending or a cut in taxes will be multiplied as its influence spreads through the economy and the various interconnections and feedbacks operate. We recall that the large macro-econometric models are still unable to agree on the size of the multiplier, despite the fact that Keynes developed the theoretical concept over sixty years ago.

Repeating the exercise illustrated in Figure 9.7 a large number of times gives an explanation of why conventional economic modellers are unable to agree on the impacts of changes in government policy on the economy, an issue discussed in Chapter 7.

In general in the large, conventional models, the precise state of the economy when the stimulus is given makes little difference to their estimate of the multiplier. But our model gives a wide range of estimates of the size of the multiplier, which varies according to the state of the economy when the stimulus is applied. The short-term multiplier in fact varies from between 0.4 to 1.2.

Further, the impact of the stimulus varies even more if it is allowed to influence not just the aggregate output variable, but the overall state of sentiment as well. As far as the latter is concerned, government intervention could work either way. It could reinforce the impact of the stimulus positively if firms felt that the overall prospects for the economy were enhanced by it, or it could induce greater pessimism about the future if companies believed that it would have an adverse effect – for example, by causing more inflation.

Presumably, in reality, different mixtures of these two reactions have obtained at different points in time. If we allow for overall sentiment to be reinforced positively by the same magnitude as aggregate output and, at the other extreme, for it to be influenced negatively by the same amount, our estimate of the multiplier varies from as much as 1.8 to -0.3.

In short, the impact of government intervention varies in subtle ways depending upon the state of the economy and upon its influence not just on output but on the degree of optimism or pessimism which firms have about the future.

Nevertheless government does have a potentially very strong role in this model. If the authorities do succeed in engineering a *long-term* rise in the level of overall optimism, the average growth rate of the economy, around which cycles will still exist, will be higher. In other words, while governments cannot really influence the short term in any meaningful way, by stepping back and taking a more detached view, much more may be achieved.

The business cycle is one of the two most pervasive and important characteristics of the Western market economies. Our model, deceptively simple in mathematical terms and based upon the idea that the behaviour of individuals can be influenced directly by the behaviour of others, captures the subtleties of the deep, underlying structure of actual business cycle data. This approach outperforms decisively the account of business cycles given by conventional economics, and explains many of the failings of the orthodox approach.

Once again, the basic principles of our ants model offer new insights into a complex economic problem.

CHAPTER 10

The Wealth of Nations

The economies of the West appear in many ways to be rather diverse. But they share two key features which distinguish them from all other types of economic organization in the history of the world. As we have seen, there are persistent cycles in the rate of growth – the endless sequence of booms and recessions with which we are all familiar. And, perhaps even more strikingly, the cycles take place against a background of slow but steady underlying growth.

It is the long-term growth of the Western economies which is the topic of both this and the next two chapters. In this short chapter, the key facts about growth are discussed, along with some of the conceptual problems involved in measuring it.

Figure 10.1 plots the level of national income per head in the United

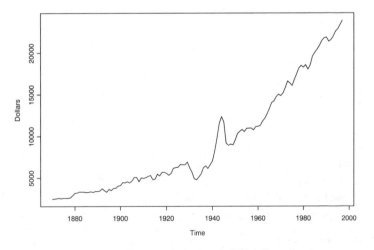

FIGURE 10.1 Real per capita income in US dollars 1870–1997

States from 1870 to 1997, after stripping out the effects of inflation. The basic data used in Figure 10.1 is the same as that of Figure 8.2 on p. 113. There, the chart used the data to plot the annual rate of growth of the US economy, of American national income per head, over time. Figure 10.1 shows the *level* of national income per head.

The average increase each year is small, being under 2 per cent, but the cumulative effect is dramatic. Most of the short-term business cycles register in the chart as no more than minor wriggles of the line. Even the Great Depression of the 1930s and the massive expansion of the economy during the Second World War are outweighed by the steady but inexorable underlying growth. During the course of the twentieth century, American national income per head has risen from under $5,000, in today's money, to almost $25,000.

In terms of the absolute level of national income, the United States was the richest country in the world in the early years of the century, and has remained so throughout.* In Western Europe, for example, the present levels of per capita national income are in the range $15,000–$20,000.

But in terms of the average long-term growth *rate*, the experience of the United States is entirely typical of the Western economies, most of which have per capita incomes that have grown by around 2 per cent a year during the twentieth century.

The American figure is 1.8 per cent, while in both France and Germany it is 1.9 per cent. There are only a few exceptions to the 2 per cent rule. At the top of the range, Japanese growth averaged 3 per cent a year, transforming the country during the course of the century from a very poor one, where living standards were well below those of much of South America, to a rich one. At the bottom, Australia, New Zealand and the UK are all just under 1.5 per cent, the first two because of a long-term decline in commodity prices and the UK because of its long-standing problems, only recently solved, associated with being the first country to industrialize.

The concentration of average growth rates around the figure of 2 per cent a year is really quite remarkable, given the diverse historical

---

* There are occasional exceptions to this statement. Countries whose wealth is based on the production of primary commodities or agriculture, such as Australia in the 1900s and some Middle Eastern states in the 1970s have sometimes overtaken the US, but only temporarily.

experience of the countries which now constitute the developed world. Capitalism has succeeded against a background of an enormously wide variety of political regimes and institutions. Even liberal democracy does not appear to be a necessary condition for capitalism to take root and prosper, judging by the circumstances under which Japan first developed, or by the various experiences of Germany in the first half of this century and of East Asian countries, despite their recent setback, in the last few decades.

In some circles it is fashionable to be sceptical of economic growth, but the process steadily and surely transforms the prospects of individuals and nations. Think of Britain in 1914, at the onset of the First World War, controller of the largest empire ever seen, before or since, on which the sun never set, and whose economic strength underpinned the most powerful set of armed forces in history to that date. Britain's industry produced half as much again as either of her main European rivals, France and Germany. The comparison of output and standards of living across countries with different tastes and traditions, even at the same point in time, is fraught with difficulties,*　but the diligent and painstaking efforts of economic historians suggest that in the mid-1990s, the total amount of goods and services produced on the island of Taiwan exceeds that of Britain at the height of her imperial power.

Closer to home, the benefits of economic growth, even at a slow rate, when sustained over time are readily apparent. Many readers will have personal recollections, of pleasure or distaste, of the decade of the 1960s. A dry economic statistic is that since then, average material standards of living in Western Europe and America have doubled.

This change is constantly seen in our everyday lives. Ownership of cars, and even telephones, in the Europe of the 1960s was confined to a distinct minority of households. Refrigerators, washing machines and spin-dryers were still luxuries, beyond the reach of many, and the families of Northern Europe, lacking central heating, huddled in their living rooms in the bleak winter evenings, as their forefathers had done since

---

* A reflection of the changing nature of the economy over time is that for much of the nineteenth century, the British census, under the heading 'occupation', included a category entitled 'gentleman, rentier or capitalist'. Perhaps the wheel has now come full circle and it is time for this tradition to be re-instated.

time immemorial. Products such as videos, CD players and personal computers had not been invented. The four *nouveaux riches* Yorkshiremen in the famous Monty Python comedy sketch proclaimed their humble origins and the benefits of material deprivation: 'Ah were 'appier then, though we were poor – *because* we were poor!', but they were careful to do so after a splendid dinner, while sipping an exclusive claret. Money does matter.

Over a longer time-perspective, the lives of the comfortable middle classes in the early nineteenth century, portrayed in the novels of writers such as Jane Austen, illuminate our present prosperity. Seemingly inexplicable diseases could carry off, without warning, even the wealthy. Travel anywhere outside the immediate neighbourhood of town or village was lengthy and uncomfortable. More trivially, an event such as the purchase of a new dress was something to be anticipated and savoured, rather than being the casual outcome of a weekend trip to the out-of-town shopping centre.

The typical rise of around 2 per cent a year in average living standards may not seem to make much difference from one year to the next, but over the course of a decade or so it becomes noticeable. In contrast, for almost the whole of human history, a sustained increase of 2 per cent took not a year but decades to achieve. There were marked fluctuations in living standards, both from year to year and even from century to century. But in societies dominated by agriculture, these were mainly due to the vicissitudes of the weather, which determined the productivity of agriculture and the size of the harvest. Advances were made in knowledge and technology which helped improve the agricultural yield, but these were few and far between and could take literally centuries to spread from one country to another. The basis of progress was insecure and fragile, and for very long periods prosperity could and did fall. Indeed, the material circumstances of the average Roman in the second century AD were arguably higher than those of a typical citizen anywhere in the world until the seventeenth or even eighteenth century.

The West recovered extremely slowly following the collapse of the Roman Empire, and the authoritative work of Angus Maddison suggests that in the 1000 years between AD 500 and 1500, the volume of overall economic activity rose to three times its initial level. But to put this in perspective, the Western economies grew as much in percentage terms in the twenty years following 1950, and the absolute increase in the volume of goods and services produced was obviously much greater, given the enormously higher starting point. Growth appears to have begun to accelerate in Western Europe around 1500. Controversies about its subsequent actual rate, up to and including the first half of the nineteenth century, rage amongst economic historians.

It should be said in passing that arguments about measuring the exact rate at which an economy is growing are not merely of antiquarian interest. Estimates of the total size of an economy cannot be made as in a scientific experiment – it cannot be placed on a pair of scales to be weighed! The evidence must be pieced together, using information about how much people are being paid from income tax files, or about how much is being spent in the shops from the revenue from taxes on spending such as VAT, and from a myriad of other bits of material.

Estimates of the total amount which is being either spent or produced are made, not surprisingly, in money terms. So in 1997 the total size of the British economy is estimated to have been over £700 billion (around $1,200 billion), and that of the United States to have been some $8,000 billion. There is then a separate and crucial task to be carried out. From year to year the money value of an economy can increase purely because of inflation. We might imagine a hypothetical situation in which exactly the same amounts of goods and services were produced from one year to the next, but the price of everything went up by 5 per cent a year. This economy would grow in money terms by 5 per cent, but in reality nothing would have changed, for identical amounts of things are produced each year. So the growth in the size of the economy in money terms from year to year has to be split into two components. The part which is due simply to inflation, to higher prices, and the part which represents a genuine increase in the amount which is produced. Economists speak of the latter as the 'real' growth rate, a specialized use of the word 'real' which can cause confusion to non-economists. But, clearly, it is the real growth rate which counts.

Apportioning the growth rate in money terms into 'real' and 'inflation' parts is by no means straightforward, for products change from year to year. We may be duly sceptical of the extent to which, say, a new variant of a brand of washing powder really is different from last year's offer, but there are obvious and dramatic differences in products such as CD players, video recorders and personal computers. Deciding the real growth rate of this kind of product is not easy, for the very nature of the product alters rapidly. It is certainly arguable that, because of such changes, in recent years Western economies have grown more rapidly than official data suggest.

In contrast, environmentalists argue that the real rate of growth of the developed economies has been over-estimated in recent decades. The decision as to what should and should not be counted as part of the economy in official national estimates is governed by a set of conventions which were developed in the 1930s and 1940s. These can lead to rather obvious anomalies. Suppose, for example, that a woman stays at home rather than going out to work, and, acting on some curious whim, decides to wash all her family's clothes by hand. This act adds value to the economy: previously the clothes were dirty, but now they are clean and the members of the family can go about their business without offending their colleagues through their personal hygiene. But the chore of washing the clothes is not counted as part of the overall economy, essentially because no price is charged for it. The task takes place within the household rather than the market economy. If the same woman went out to work, and used her wages to send the laundry to the dry cleaners, the effect on the clothes would be the same. They were dirty, they become clean. But because a price is paid in this case, the process of cleaning the clothes is counted as part of the real economy.

The purpose of this example is not to hold up the methodology of national income accounting to ridicule, for any criteria are to some extent arbitrary and will create anomalies. And, whatever the particular problems, our personal experiences are very much in line with what the national accounts statistics tell us. For most of us, our material prosperity is higher than it was twenty years ago, and the official statistics tell us that the real economy has grown over this period.

The environmentalists' point is more serious. Their arguments, it should be said, have been very much assisted by the work of economists, who are only too aware of the sometimes arbitrary nature of the conventions used in national accounts. As long ago as 1971, Nobel prizewinner James Tobin and his colleague William Nordhaus proposed a series of adjustments to the standard criteria used to measure the size of the American economy. Commuting into work, for example, by car or by train is counted as adding to the size of the economy, because money is spent in the process on train tickets, petrol and the like. But most people (except perhaps some of those from English boarding schools where a taste for masochism is acquired early in life) would wish to avoid the process of commuting altogether if they could. For them it has negative value. So one potential adjustment to conventional ways of measuring the size of the economy would be to put a negative price on the time spent commuting, and deduct this from the estimate of the total amount of output.

The main worries for environmentalists are that the costs of pollution are not measured in the national accounts, and that insufficient emphasis is placed on the degree to which the whole process of economic activity reduces the potentially limited stock of resources such as fossil fuels.

The practical problem of incorporating such effects is that this, too, involves a further set of somewhat arbitrary assumptions. For example, it is not clear whether pollution in the developed world has increased or fallen in the past fifty years. New forms have arisen, such as those associated with motor vehicles, which impinge upon the population as a whole. But pollution which mainly affected the more working-class areas of a country, such as the smoke and effluents from industrial production, has declined dramatically, both as old industries have closed down and as legislation on matters such as clean air has taken effect.

Despite the practical problems of measurement, these are serious and legitimate concerns. Indeed, the statistical arm of the European Commission, Eurostat, has been investigating the question intensively in recent years. But it does seem to be the case that, even when allowance is made for such factors, growth in the West has still been positive in recent decades.

To return, however, to the general theme of economic growth. During the eighteenth century, in the countries of Northern Europe, and in particular Britain and the Netherlands, growth began to accelerate to the point where its effects became clearly discernible, particularly during the course of an adult lifetime. The absolute rate of growth was not at all high, at most one per cent a year, but the changes in technology and the gradual build-up of fixed capital in machines and factories were noticeable.

This entirely new phenomenon of a marked expansion in the size of the economy quite independently of the state of the harvest, excited the interest of a group of great thinkers. Adam Smith, whose work is the basis for a great deal of modern economics, published his masterpiece in 1776, entitled *An Inquiry into the Nature and Causes of the Wealth of Nations*. A few years later, Thomas Malthus thought hard about the question of growth, and came to his famous, but mistaken, conclusion that the process would eventually be overwhelmed by the problems of over-population.

In the early decades of the nineteenth century, David Ricardo, who we came across briefly in Chapter 7, addressed the question of economic growth. His early death, at the age of fifty-one, is, incidentally, a succinct illustration of the immense difference between life in the West today and in the early nineteenth century. Despite being one of the richest men in the country, he could not buy the antibiotics which would have prevented a minor ear infection from developing into a fatal illness, for the very good reason that they did not exist.

Ricardo's main work, *The Principles of Political Economy*, appeared in 1819, and covers a wide range of questions, such as why nations trade with each other and the impact of trade on prosperity, and the problem, highly salient at the time given the enormous cost to the British government of financing the major military struggles against Napoleon, of whether or not the way in which governments finance any gap between their expenditure and their receipts from taxation makes any difference to the economy.

One of his main fascinations was with the new phenomenon of economic growth, and whether it could be sustained in the long run. He regarded the distribution of national income between wages and profits as being of fundamental importance, and worried that various forces would eventually become so powerful they would undermine profitability and hence bring growth to a halt.

Writing some thirty years after Ricardo, Marx was probably the first political economist (as all the early thinkers thought of themselves) to see that the unprecedented economic growth generated by the emerging capitalist system of production was permanent rather than transient. His explicitly political writings – a mixture of the sentimental, the messianic and the merely tendentious – should not overshadow this great insight which he had as an economist. He believed that the progress of technology, and its physical embodiment in new machines, would guarantee growth in the long run, even though its progress would be subject to wild fluctuations.

It is of course possible that Marx's economic analysis would have been even more convincing if he had taken to heart the lament of his mother, which he recalled sadly on the occasion of his birthday in 1868. 'If only', she had written to a relative, 'little Karl had made some capital rather than just writing about it.'*

But the relevant point for us is not so much the precise arguments which these early economists put forward, and whether or not with the benefit of hindsight we can judge them to have been right or wrong. It is that they each in their own way regarded an understanding of the process of growth as being absolutely central to the emerging discipline of economics. Growth was by far the most striking feature which distinguished industrial capitalism from all previous social and economic systems, and it was therefore essential to try to explain it.

Within economics, however, as we saw in Chapter 5, a remarkable intellectual phenomenon emerged during the second half of the nineteenth century. The emphasis switched from thinking about how growth was generated in the first place, to the question of how best to allocate the proceeds of growth, which were simply assumed to be given. Perhaps the most bizarre aspect of this shift of emphasis in economics was that the question of what actually generated economic growth remained unsolved.

In a true science, a problem will stretch the minds of the very ablest. Once explained, understanding will initially be confined to the select few, and then gradually be disseminated to lower and lower levels. An example is the theory of relativity, a major breakthrough in the early decades of this century, but one whose key results are now accessible even to the

---

* I am grateful to James Buchan for this excellent – and true – story.

intelligent lay person through titles such as *Einstein for Beginners*. But with economic growth, this did not happen. The question remained unanswered. This defining characteristic of capitalism, the one which sets it apart from all other previously or currently existing economic systems, was not a matter of concern in mainstream economic theory for the best part of a century. Awareness of the problem did not vanish completely, but it was of very much secondary importance compared to the challenge of developing and refining the theoretical model of how best to allocate a given quantity of resources among individual consumers and individual companies – the theory of competitive or general equilibrium.

Our ants may be able to shed a bit of light on this curious intellectual development, for the world of academic economics is by no means immune from the trends of fashion. Subjects are often studied for no other reason than that others are doing so. As Ralph W. Emerson remarked over a hundred years ago, 'If you would know what nobody knows, read what everyone reads, just one year afterwards,' though the time lag involved in economic theory is considerably longer. Having been neglected for a long period of time, growth theory suddenly became very fashionable, the hot property for graduate students, in the 1960s and early 1970s. It then suffered a relapse, before coming back into prominence towards the end of the 1980s. Exactly what economics has had to say about growth in these two periods is the topic of the next chapter.

CHAPTER 11

To Have and Have Not

For most of this chapter, our ants are conspicuous by their absence, since it is concerned with how conventional economics has, in recent decades, attempted to explain the sustained, long-term growth in the Western economies. Ants, as we might expect, simply do not come into their stories.

The question of explaining the growth of the Western market economies did not really re-emerge in economic theory until the 1940s. Thinkers such as Schumpeter considered the problem at length before then. He used the memorable phrase 'gales of creative destruction' to describe the process of innovation and technical change which, while it can and does destroy whole industries, is a crucial factor in our current prosperity. But his work has never been absorbed into economic theory. Keynes, for all his doubts about and criticisms of mainstream economics, and for all his prominence as an economist, never addressed the issue of long-term growth.

Initially, theoretical forays back into the topic were made by economists who were, to varying degrees, sceptical of the prevailing orthodoxy. It was not until 1956 that a clearly articulated account in the conventional tradition appeared. The American Robert Solow, subsequently the recipient of the Nobel Prize, published an article modestly entitled 'A Contribution to the Theory of Economic Growth'. It is one of the few articles which can be genuinely described as 'seminal', for it has given rise to an enormous literature and is an undoubted intellectual *tour de force*.

Solow's key idea, like so many really original ones, is extremely simple. The basis of his model is what is described in the jargon as a 'production function'. This is a straightforward mathematical formula which relates the total amount of output produced in an economy to two inputs, the stock of accumulated physical capital goods (machinery, computers, and the like) and labour.

It is very much a theory of what takes place at the overall level of the economy, rather than at the level of the individual firm. The approach offers an account of what happens to the aggregate amount of output produced when the total stock of capital and/or the labour force are increased by specific amounts. It is assumed that, in the background, is an economy which consists of an enormous number of very small firms. But the link between this and what happens at the aggregate level has never been resolved in a realistic way.

Increases in output are brought about by increases in the amounts of capital or labour which are used. In addition, Solow introduced a third factor into his model, namely technological progress. Technology is assumed to improve at a constant rate each year, which enables both labour and capital to be more productive – machines and workers become better over time as well as there being more of them.

The model is a highly abstract description of reality, for in the actual world many different kinds of goods and services are produced, the contribution which different kinds of machines make to output varies, and the quality of individual workers is by no means the same. In the Solow model, these practical difficulties are assumed away, and it is as if there were only one kind of output, one kind of machinery, and all workers are identical.

This in itself is not necessarily a problem for the model. In drawing a map, we have to make simplifications of reality, and provided that we represent the key features, it serves its purpose well. In fact, forty years on, conventional economics has not come up with a decisively better account of the process of economic growth than that provided by Solow.

This is not to say that the model gives a good account of reality. Indeed, as we shall see, its implications are distinctly at odds with some key aspects of the actual experience of growth observed around the world.

The essential problems of the Solow model are two-fold. First, no explanation is given as to why technical progress takes place. Technology is simply assumed, in the words of one critic, 'to fall from the sky like manna from Heaven'.

The second problem is more subtle, and concerns the specific relation-ship which is assumed between the inputs, capital and labour, and the level of output. There are, in turn, two aspects to this. First, the implications for the amount by which output is increased if the amounts of both labour and capital are increased by the same percentage. Second, what happens to output if either of the two inputs on its own is increased.

If the amounts of capital and labour employed both increase by, say, 1 per cent, then the amount of output produced in the Solow model will also rise by 1 per cent. The formula exhibits what are known as 'constant returns to scale'. Regardless of how much capital and labour are already employed, a 1 per cent increase in both these inputs will lead to a constant 1 per cent increase in output, whereas an increase of 1 per cent in either capital or labour on its own leads to a less than 1 per cent increase in output – to decreasing, or diminishing, returns to scale. This may seem at first sight rather odd, but the rationale is as follows.

Suppose that the increase in the labour force were zero. This is in fact close to being a practical reality in much of the West. Imagine what the effect would be of providing more and more of the *same kind* of capital equipment to a fixed number of workers. In a factory, for example, a worker may be able to look after several machines at once. But, after a certain point, each extra machine provided will make less and less difference to his or her output, as the task of coping with them and keeping them all running smoothly becomes harder and harder. Eventually, the addition of a further machine will make no difference at all to the amount produced, because the worker, even one of the fabled Stakhanovites of Stalin's Soviet Union, will have no time to operate it.

In other words, expansion of the capital stock implies a decline in the return on further expansion. Eventually, for this reason, growth may ultimately cease. Solow resolved this potential problem by introducing the third element, technical progress, into his model. And, as we have seen, no reason is given in the model as to why this progress takes place – it just happens.

So, ultimately, growth in the Solow model is not explained by the model at all. It seems that over the course of time, as societies get richer, population growth slows and eventually becomes zero. For a period, expansion of the labour force can still take place as more and more women decide to work. But this process cannot go on indefinitely. Eventually, the growth in the labour force cannot be greater than zero. Against such a background, the Solow model implies that further increases in the capital stock lead to smaller and smaller additions to output. Further sustained growth can only take place because of the Third Man of the Solow model, technical progress.

The concepts of diminishing or constant returns to scale are a key foundation not just of the Solow growth model, but of the whole corpus of conventional economic theory. In such a world, there is no advantage to a firm in being big. Quite the contrary under diminishing returns, for then the larger the firm is, the *less* efficiently it is able to produce.

This assumption means that there are strong restrictions on the ability to reinforce any competitive advantage which might arise. In practice, companies will strive hard to do just this, whether through improving the technique and organization of production, the purchase of supplies, the structure of the distribution outlets for the firm's products, the marketing process, or whatever. But in a world of diminishing returns, such efforts are ultimately futile. After a certain point, the cost of making each additional unit of production rises. By definition, discounts are not available for bulk purchase of supplies. Efficient national and international channels of distribution and marketing, in which companies can take advantage of being big, are assumed not to exist. In such a world, competitive advantage cannot persist.

It may be thought that the actual structures of capitalist economies, dominated as they are by enormous firms, would be regarded as an empirical refutation of this view of the world. This apparently glaring gap between theory and reality is presumably one of the reasons why many students abandon the discipline after their initial acquaintance with it in Introductory Economics.* There is much to be said for this opinion. But the orthodox have an astute defence, which is intellectually coherent if far from convincing. It is 'as if' markets operate as though there are many small firms and the conditions of a competitive market exist. Actual firms may well be huge, but if one were making excessive profits in a particular market, other large companies have the financial power and resources to enter that market and ensure that those profits can no longer persist.

The assumption used by Solow of either diminishing or constant

---

* And abandon it they do. The numbers of students majoring in economics has fallen dramatically in the 1990s throughout the Anglo-Saxon world.

returns fits in very nicely with standard economic theory, for it is essential to derive the basic theorems of free-market economics. The mathematics simply do not give the same kinds of results with increasing returns, when there are advantages to being big, and when successive increases of inputs into the process of production lead to larger and larger increases in output.

This world of economic theory contrasts sharply with that of our ants. In the former, negative feedback predominates and any differences between firms tend to be smoothed away. In the latter, positive feedback is a decisive force. The emulation of the activities of others leads to trends being reinforced rather than reversed. Indeed, as we saw in Chapter 2, in some variants of the ants model, such as those used to analyse industrial location or the struggle between competing high-tech products, the reinforcement can persist for very long periods of time.

The response of economists to the Solow model in the first two decades of its existence was a case of, as Sherlock Holmes put it, the dog that did not bark. In the natural sciences, confronted by a new and elegant theory from a distinguished member of the profession, the first instinct of many would be to try to test the theory empirically. In other words, to confront the properties and implications of the model with actual data from the economy, and to see if the two were in broad conformity.

The response in economics was completely different. Except in the most rudimentary sense, the model was not tested. Rather, it was assumed to be a reasonable description of reality, and was used to try to account for the sources of actual growth. A vast and increasingly sophisticated elaboration of Solow's original model filled the pages of academic economic journals. But empirical testing remained noticeable by its absence.

An esoteric debate did take place, led by economists at Cambridge University, in which the Solow model was attacked, not on empirical grounds, but on a mixture of ideological and theoretical points. The exact details of this argument, to which I was subjected at inordinate length as a student at Cambridge in the early 1970s, need not concern us here. In comparison, the medieval theological wrangles about how many angels could stand on the end of a pin appear positively illuminating. It was, however, held that the Solow model attempted to provide an intellectual justification for the existence of profits. Some of the finest minds in economics diverted their energies into trying to show that profits could not be justified in this way. One figure above all was revered. Piero Sraffa, an old Stalinist Fellow of Trinity College, had published virtually nothing for over thirty years, until his masterpiece appeared, the enigmatically entitled *Production of Commodities by Means of Commodities*. In one of Evelyn Waugh's novels, the hero is plagued by voices, which he imagines are being broadcast by fellow passengers on his ship. In a futile effort to distract them, he takes from the ship's library and reads aloud the most boring book he can imagine, Charles Kingsley's *Westward Ho!* Had Sraffa's book been available, he would certainly have succeeded in his task.

In mainstream economics, however, a whole new literature grew up, known as growth accounting, which *assumed* that the Solow model was broadly correct, and apportioned the actual growth over time in Western economies to the three explanatory factors in the model, namely the size of the capital stock and labour force, and technological progress. Because there is no readily available measure of how rapidly the latter is changing, the contributions of capital and labour were measured, and subtracted from the actual growth rate which had been achieved. This difference was assumed, by definition, to be due to technical progress.

Studies showed quite clearly that by far the biggest contribution to Western economic growth, according to the growth-accounting approach, was made by technology. In other words, growth remained largely unexplained by economics, since in this model, technical progress was simply assumed to happen, quite independently of the rate of investment or the growth in the labour force. Some scholars, at least, felt that this conclusion was not completely satisfactory, and intensive efforts were made, essentially within the same intellectual framework, to try to see if the result could be altered.

But by the mid-1970s, interest in growth theory began to wane. Nothing had really been resolved, but it was no longer felt to be at the intellectual cutting edge of the discipline. In the mid-1980s, a new generation of American economists revisited the problem. And this time round, a whole new emphasis was placed on empirical testing, on whether the properties of theoretical models conformed to the facts. This habit has by no means spread throughout the economics profession, even within the United States, and the old habit of regarding theories as being *a priori* correct still persists on a wide scale, but this group of economists has exercised a powerful and beneficial influence on the subject in a number of areas, by insisting on the need to provide at least some initial credibility for a theoretical model by comparing it with the facts.

Even in the physical sciences, the testing of theories often proves to be a difficult and demanding task. One of the predictions of Einstein's theories, for example, is that light rays are bent by the gravitational force of the sun. But it was many years before a successful experiment could be carried out which would test this hypothesis. Some of the methods devised to test aspects of quantum theory are, of themselves, considerable feats of ingenuity.

The problems are compounded in economics by the fact that it is usually impossible to repeat an experiment. After all, America has only one history, and so we only have one data series for economic growth over the years in the United States. We cannot, by whatever means, construct another. We do, of course, have data on growth over time in different countries apart from the United States, which is certainly of assistance, but even so the amount of data available is strictly limited and is non-replicable.

The evidence which we do have of growth rates in different countries creates serious problems for Solow-type models. A clear prediction of such models is that standards of living around the world should converge in the long run, for two reasons.

First, and probably the more important, is that technology is universally available and applicable. Within the strict confines of the model, technical progress simply advances at a steady rate year on year, and the entire stock of knowledge is readily accessible to anyone. If this is the case, any country can equip its factories and workers with the best technology in the world. This assumption of the sheer availability of technology is by no means unreasonable as an approximation to reality. Certain kinds of knowledge may be protected by patents for limited periods of time, but in general information is widely disseminated.* Even

---

* More and more so with the growth of the Internet. The positive and welcoming attitude of the American government to it contrasts with the bizarre view of the European Commission. Powerful elements in the Commission want to tax every single bit of information which is exchanged over the Net. O Gosplan, thou shouldst be living at this hour!

the most highly protected secrets, such as American military technology, usually became available to the Soviet Union, albeit by clandestine means.

The second reason for convergence of living standards in orthodox growth models is the assumption of diminishing returns to the capital stock. As more and more investment takes place, the extra output produced becomes smaller and smaller. The implication is that poor countries, starting off with a capital stock which is small relative to the size of the economy, will grow rapidly, and rich countries will grow much more slowly. So poor countries will catch up.

Theoretical economics makes liberal use of the phrase 'in the long run', and a perennial practical question is 'How long is the long run?' A contemporary of mine experienced a devastating practical illustration of its importance shortly after he had been elected as an economics fellow of an Oxford college in the mid-1970s. The college had been left a large sum of money, and the fellows gathered to decide how to invest it. By chance, he was the only economist present at the meeting, and was suitably nervous when the Master asked his opinion on the strategic direction of the investment, whether it should be focused on equities, bonds or land. However, he pulled himself together and argued, in a short but elegant contribution, that the money should be put into equities. The elderly Bursar – effectively the finance director – looked down his nose severely: 'I am afraid that you have no experience of these matters, for you are a very young man indeed. I have to tell you that land has served this college well as a source of investment for the last two hundred years.' My friend felt crushed. But he was saved by the intervention of the Professor of Ancient History, who began, 'But surely, Bursar, the last two hundred years are a rather unusual short period in world history.'

The last two centuries are unusual indeed, for they represent the period of existence of capitalist market economies. Orthodox models of economic growth purport to give an explanation of growth in such economies, and so it is reasonable to examine data over as much of this period as possible in order to check the plausibility of the hypothesis that incomes per head around the world will converge in the long run. It should be said that much of the recent applied literature on the convergence hypothesis only looks at data from around 1960 onwards, which seems far too restrictive.

Economic historians spend a great deal of time trying to piece together the basic facts about the past, and perhaps the most authoritative recent estimates of income per head have been made by Angus Maddison in his book *Monitoring the World Economy 1820–1992*.* The practical difficulties involved are formidable. But, unless the estimates are completely wrong, they do provide very strong evidence *against* the convergence hypothesis and hence against the empirical validity of conventional models of economic growth.

In 1870, for example, Maddison estimates that national output per head in both France and Germany was just under 80 per cent of that of the United States. And in the mid-1990s, this figure was unchanged. In other words, over the course of 125 years, the most advanced economies of Continental Europe have *not* caught up with America at all. They have grown at the same rate, but the percentage gap between American and European per capita output levels has not changed.

These comparisons can be extended more generally. Maddison in fact provides a summary of output per head in seven different regions of the world over time. The regions are pretty well self-explanatory: Western Europe, Southern Europe, Eastern Europe, Latin America, Asia and Africa. The exception is the seventh, styled 'Western Offshoots' by Maddison, and comprising the United States, Canada, Australia and New Zealand.

In the table below, we compare output per head in these regions at four dates, starting in 1820. The second date is 1913, on the eve of the First World War, and around a century after the beginning of capitalism on a world scale. The next date chosen is 1950, when normality was broadly restored following the convulsions of the Second World War, and the final date is 1992, the latest for which Maddison provides estimates for the aggregate regions.

In 1820, Western Europe was the centre of technological development in the world. The first column of Table 11.1 compares output per head in the other regions in 1820 relative to that of Western Europe. In other words, the figures given are not the estimates of the *actual* levels of income per head, but of output per head as a *percentage* of that of Western Europe. So,

---

* Published by the OECD, Paris, 1995.

for example, in 1820 output per head in the Western Offshoots is estimated to have been 90 per cent of that of Western Europe, and that of Southern Europe 60 per cent. Moving to the next row, the data for 1913, we again compare output per head of each region relative to that of Western Europe. The figure for the Western Offshoots, for example, is 140. This does not mean that output per head in this region only rose from 90 in 1820 to 140 in 1913. It tells us that in 1820 output per head in the Western Offshoot countries was 90 per cent of that of Western Europe in 1820. And in 1913, it was 140 per cent of that of Western Europe in 1913.

TABLE 11.1. Output per head as a percentage of income per head in Western Europe

Region	1820	1913	1950	1992
Western Offshoots	90	140	180	120
Southern Europe	60	45	40	50
Eastern Europe	60	45	50	25
Latin America	55	40	50	30
Asia	45	20	15	20
Africa	35	15	15	10

Source: Calculated from Maddison, *Monitoring the World Economy*, OECD, Paris, 1995

With the exception of the Western Offshoots, dominated of course by the United States, output per head in every other region of the world, *compared to* output per head in Western Europe, was lower in 1992 than it was in 1820. Everywhere else, even in Africa, the absolute levels of output per head have grown over this period, but compared to Europe they have grown less.

In 1820, Southern Europe had an output per head of 60 per cent of

Western Europe's, but of only 50 per cent in 1992. Eastern Europe, too, started at 60 per cent of Western levels, fell back to 50 per cent by 1950 and then, following their disastrous adoption of planned economies, collapsed to only 25 per cent of the West's level by 1992. In the other regions, too, compared to Western Europe, output per head fell markedly over time. The only sub-period when the less developed regions more or less held their own was between 1913 and 1950, during which Western Europe was devastated twice by world wars, as well as experiencing the greatest short-term, cyclical recession in history in the early 1930s.

In short, far from converging, over the period of 170-odd years for which data is available, output per head has diverged rather spectacularly.

Problems for the orthodox growth theory are also raised by the annual average growth rates achieved in these regions over the periods 1820–1913 and 1913–92. Broadly speaking, these represent the first and second centuries in the life of the economic system of market, capitalist economies. (For many reasons, the year 1913 represents a more natural break than the actual turn of the century, but even if we do the calculations on the basis of 1900, the conclusions are very similar.) During this time, an immense amount of capital accumulation has taken place, in machines, factories, computers, railways, airlines or whatever.

Standard growth theory predicts diminishing returns to capital investment. If this were true, we would expect growth rates in the period 1913–92 to be lower than those of 1820–1913. But this is not the case. In six out of the seven regions, growth was higher in the twentieth century than it was in the nineteenth. In Western Europe, the most developed part of the world in 1820, average annual growth was 1.9 per cent from 1820 to 1913, and 2.5 per cent from 1913 to 1992. The exception is the Western Offshoots group, where growth slowed from 4.2 per cent a year in the former period to 3.1 per cent in the latter. But this simply reflects how small the economies of this group were in the early nineteenth century. A substantial proportion of American growth in the nineteenth century came from opening up enormous parts of its territory; this, clearly, could not be repeated in the twentieth century.

Worries about the empirical validity of Solow-type growth models existed almost from their inception, but for many years these were confined to a rather disparate group of dissidents. It is only in the last decade or so that mainstream economists working on growth models have confronted the evidence openly.

The new step taken in growth theory in the past decade or so is to accept that diminishing returns are not a realistic description of the world. Instead, the concept of increasing returns has been embraced, albeit in a rather restricted and bizarre way. For old habits die hard. In the new growth theory,* individual firms are still assumed to operate with the same kinds of returns to scale posited in the Solow model. Increasing returns are encountered only at the *aggregate* level, due to what the jargon of economics describes as 'positive externalities'.

The general concept of externalities is rather smart, and represents a genuine contribution of economists to helpful ways of thinking about the world. The individual car driver, for example, gains benefits from the convenience of having his or her car, and also pays costs associated with its use, such as petrol, the purchase price of the car, repairs and so on. But using the car generates costs to other people, which are external to the individual driver and which are not captured by the market mechanism left to its own devices. Exhaust fumes create pollution, and each additional car on the road adds to the burden of traffic, and slows everyone down. But, in the absence of legislation, there is no way of allocating these costs to the driver who creates them.

This is an example of negative externalities – they make everyone else worse off. In much of the new growth literature, externalities are hypothesized to be positive. For example, it has been suggested that the overall efficiency of individual firms depends not just on its own inputs into the production process, but on the aggregate stock of capital in the economy as a whole. The rationale is that capital accumulation results in learning and emulation, which then raises efficiency in the economy as a whole.

This approach, although an important step forward intellectually, does have a somewhat contrived and artificial air about it. It is almost like the highly ingenious and ever more complicated circles of motion drawn in the Middle Ages to try to make the theory of the sun moving round the

---

* For the benefit of British readers, this is the notorious 'post neo-classical endogenous growth theory', a phrase which attracted widespread ridicule when used by the Chancellor of the Exchequer.

Earth fit the observations of actual movements. Not surprisingly, in practice these kinds of model do not work very well. Indeed, one of the instigators, Paul Roemer, has himself concluded that they cannot really be said to perform much better than the orthodox Solow-type models.

The idea, however, that a specific 'growth factor' – be it investment in people through education or training, or research and development, or public infrastructure – carries special, beneficial properties is one which Western policy-makers have found very attractive. In the earlier, orthodox view of the growth process, economic policy has no long-term effects on growth. In the new approach, subsidizing the factor which generates the positive externality can have powerful consequences. The authors of the models themselves are rather reluctant to draw strong policy conclusions, because of the uncertainty which surrounds the identification of the essential ingredient.

The theoretical discussion has moved one step further on in the last few years, and the assumption of the more general existence of increasing returns is now being taken seriously. An important way in which this is expressed is through the idea of 'growth clubs'. Groups of countries find themselves locked into a particular club, from which escape is very hard. Within each cluster, according to this theory, output per head may very well show a strong tendency to converge. But between different clusters, differences will be magnified.

This approach has the advantage of being more consistent with the evidence set out in Table 11.1. It still does not account for why differences between countries in the same club, such as the United States and Germany, can persist for over a century, but it does allow for differences between the clubs to grow.

Output per head has risen over time in all the separate groups identified in the table, but the absolute gaps between rich and moderately well-off, and between the merely comfortable and the poor, have widened dramatically. After adjusting for inflation, output per head in 1820 is estimated to have been $1,300 in Western Europe, $700 in Latin America and $450 in Africa. By 1992, these had grown to, respectively, $17,500, $4,800 and $1,300. Even allowing for an appropriate amount of scepticism about the accuracy of the earlier figures, the absolute gaps between these three 'clubs' have grown enormously.

Models which exhibit increasing returns have much in common with the world of our ants. The key characteristic they share is the tendency for effects to be self-reinforcing. The precise properties of any particular model vary according to the problem being addressed. So in the version of the ants model that explains the volatility of share prices and exchange rates, long periods of relatively stable collective behaviour are followed by large and rapid changes. The cause of both these phenomena is the self-reinforcing process of individuals altering their behaviour in the light of what others do. In our account of how products and technologies gain complete dominance of certain markets, the self-reinforcing process, once started, is far more difficult to reverse. But both rely upon the potential magnification of small changes within, or disturbances to, the system.

We now move on to see how these ideas can be applied to a theory of growth which is based, unlike conventional approaches, very firmly on individual firms and on the interactions between them.

CHAPTER 12

Great Oaks from Little Acorns

An economy can only grow at the overall level if the individual firms of which it is comprised grow. So any theory of growth should be based upon the activity and behaviour of individual companies. In the same way, with our ants an explanation of the behaviour of the colony as a whole can only be given by a theory based upon the behaviour of the individual ants which make up the society. In contrast, orthodox economics relies upon hypothetical regularities between the total amount of inputs used in the production process at the aggregate level, and the resulting amount of output which emerges.

As with Dante's Seven Circles of Hell, economists have a keenly developed sense of the relative wickedness of different types of intellectual sinners, of deviants from the true faith. Apostate economists are unequivocally confined to the lowest depths of all. But it is still a matter of debate as to whether the next level is occupied by sociologists or by the denizens of business schools.

It might be thought that much common cause would exist between economists and scholars in business schools. After all, both are apparently concerned with how companies operate. But this is far from the case. Economists regard business schools partly with fear, for more and more students are opting for business studies courses rather than straight economics, and partly with contempt. Business studies is often seen by economists as a soft option, as being merely descriptive and, horror of horrors, of lacking theoretical content.

Certainly, compared to the logical rigour of much economic theory, couched as it is in the language of mathematics, the analytical content of business studies is, in general, low. And it is easy to ridicule some of the extravagant claims which are made for 'management' books. But the great strength of the serious work of business schools is that it provides detailed empirical accounts of how companies actually operate.

All theories and models are simplifications of reality. But the conventional view of growth misses out far too much. Companies do not grow simply by investing in new equipment, taking on more workers and applying new technology. These can be important, but far more is involved. Firms form alliances, carry out strategies to drive out competition, merge with or acquire other companies. They pay close attention to the organization of production, to advertising, promotion, brand image, to the sourcing of their supplies and to the distribution of their products.

Firms are driven by profits, and are constantly striving to reap the benefits of increasing returns in all aspects of their activities. Higher sales do not simply give the potential for greater efficiency and lower costs per unit of output in the process of production, they give more command over suppliers, the ability to negotiate better terms, they increase the possibility of taking over a rival, and so on.

Of course, this does not mean that large companies can never fail. Management, for example, could make a very serious mistake, or might not respond quickly enough to gradually changing patterns of consumer demand. The American car industry in the 1970s, which for decades had dominated the world, is an example of such risks. The domestic market was traditionally made up of very large, gas-guzzling saloons, transporting the conventional nuclear family of mother, father and children around. From the perspective of Detroit, small cars were for pinko Europeans and weirdos from California. But the social structure of the world was changing, as divorce rates rose, twenty-somethings postponed marriage and children, leading to smaller households and a bigger demand for small cars. Eventually, of course, Detroit responded, but not without some severe scares along the way.

In the 1990s, much of Japanese manufacturing industry, the envy of the world, has not responded adequately to a deep-seated problem. A great deal of Japan's success has been based upon the production of consumer durables, televisions, videos, washing machines and so on. But there are limits to how many of these gadgets a household wants. A second or even third video player can easily be accommodated, but where does one put the fourth or fifth – in the bathroom or the lavatory? It makes more sense to most people to stop at two or three. The failure of the Japanese to perceive this in time is an important reason underlying their current economic problems.*

Increasing returns do not characterize every aspect of economic activity. For example, one of the attractions to many consumers of a fine claret is precisely its scarcity value, the fact that so little of it can be made. The intrinsic quality of the wine is important, but sipping a *premier grand cru* in the Savoy would lose some of its savour if it were possible to produce the wine on a large, industrial scale.

And in many areas of business, there are limits to the benefits of becoming larger and larger. Sometimes these restrictions are physical. Ships of several million tonnes, for example, would convey goods across the world more efficiently than smaller, existing ones. But such ships are not built, in part because of the difficulty of finding harbours to accommodate them, and in part because of the need for large amounts of infrastructure in a port to unload them in a reasonable space of time. Organizational problems can arise in very large companies, as co-ordination and implementation of high-level decisions become more difficult. Or there may be constraints arising from anti-trust legislation on how big a particular firm is allowed to become.

But, in general, in the real world of business, increasing returns to scale are pervasive. Size does matter. The existence of this phenomenon, of the potential advantages which are conferred on an individual firm by its size, should be recognized in any plausible theory of economic growth.

Companies themselves for at least a century have shown a distinct preference for being big. In the United States, *Fortune* magazine produces an annual list of the largest companies by sales.† The precise composition of the list varies from year to year, but even the company ranked number 500, the 500th largest, in the list is massive, with annual sales of around $3 billion, and the company at number 100 has sales around $15 billion. Yet the top 100 firms usually have total sales

---

* America, in contrast, has specialized more and more in services, where it is far harder to see limits to demand. Both Wall Street and Hollywood make huge amounts for the US economy. And even Las Vegas plays a part. Why go to the effort of actually making things when Asians and Arabs can be separated from vast sums of money by simply dealing out a few playing cards?

† Gross sales are not the same as the concept of value added which is used in the national accounts to measure the total amount of output used in an economy.

considerably larger than all of the 400 ranked in positions 101–500 put together. And the top 10 companies have total sales greater than those of all the companies ranked between 101 and 200.

In terms of the total number of companies the overwhelming majority are very small. And there are arguments about whether the share of the very largest companies in total output has been rising or falling in recent years. But the tendency amongst large companies themselves is to become bigger and bigger. Indeed, 1997 saw a record year for mergers and acquisitions, involving companies to the value of almost $1 trillion in America alone. Heading the list was the $42 billion acquisition of MCI by World Com, with several mergers of companies valued at over $10 billion, such as Nations Bank and Barnett Banks and Starwood Hotels and Resorts ITT.

As a very brief diversion, it must be said that our ants have something to offer in understanding the waves of mergers and acquisitions which take place from time to time. For it does appear to be very much a fashion-related phenomenon amongst top management and the financial markets. The beginning of the century saw what was probably the biggest in world history, when many of today's giant corporations first took shape. In the 1920s, a further rapid consolidation took place, but the next period of major activity was not until the 1960s. Mergers and acquisitions take place every year, but for long periods of time the scale is low, punctuated by periods of enormous change when the system moves to a huge level of activity in this area. Thinking back to our very first chart, Figure 1.1, this pattern of behaviour looks very familiar indeed. The principles of our ants model seem relevant to any explanation of the irregular timings of merger activity. But the orthodox prefer, as in the major finance textbook by Richard Brearly and Stewart Myers, to regard these waves as a 'great unsolved mystery'. And in any event, the structure of the timing is not our concern here.

The distribution of the size of firms does have a very distinctive qualitative pattern. In part this arises through the gains which arise over time from increasing returns, from the operation of positive feedback. The bigger and more successful a firm is, the more likely it is to have these qualities enhanced. And in part the size distribution is accounted for by mergers between and acquisitions of firms.

The actual distribution is not easy to characterize with a single mathematical statistic, but its broad shape is readily recognizable. As the distinguished Cambridge economist Joan Robinson once remarked, an elephant might be hard to describe, but everyone knows one when they see it. There are a small number of extremely large firms, which are big even in relation to the group of firms immediately below them, which in turn are both themselves enormous in absolute size and relative to the group below them. This pattern is repeated as we move down in size amongst the largest firms in an economy, until we find an extremely long tail, as it were, consisting of huge numbers of very small firms.

Given that growth arises from the activities of individual companies, this suggests another desirable feature of any theory of economic growth which is even partially realistic. Over time, the theoretical model should lead to a size distribution of the individual firms within it which has similar qualitative features to the real world.

Evidence from the previous chapter about the outcome of economic growth across the world over the past 125 years or so indicates two key features which any theoretical model should have. First, there is the important notion of growth clubs. In other words, groups of countries which start off with similar conditions tend to move together over time, to stay within their club. And, second, the initial differences between clubs are certainly not eroded over time, and may even be magnified.

Further desirable features of any theoretical model of growth were discussed earlier in this chapter. Increasing returns should certainly figure in some way, as should the tendency of firms to become bigger by merging with or acquiring other companies. Above all, however, it should be based, as with our ants, upon the behaviour of individual agents. For it is firms which create growth, not aggregate economies.

Peter Allen, a former theoretical physicist now based at Cranfield University in the UK, has developed a nice way of thinking about the growth of regions or cities. Imagine a three-dimensional diagram, the floor of which is criss-crossed by lines which divide it into individual squares, or cells as we could call them, as on a chess or chequers board. In the case of a city or a region, each individual cell can readily be interpreted as corresponding to a particular geographical location.

The board can be used to play an interesting game, which is started by choosing a cell at random, and placing in it some economic activity, of small size. All the cells are blank to begin with, but can be populated as the game progresses. In chess or chequers, a series of moves is played by White or Black alternately, but in sequence. Here, the sequence can be thought of as a period of time, such as a year or whatever. As we move from period to period, the rules of the game tell us how to change both the cells which are occupied, and the heights of the cells.

In terms of the evolution of cities or of regions, the game has much in common with the world of our ants. It is based at the micro-level, for its rules tell us how each individual cell, or location, evolves by interacting with its immediate neighbours and, in principle, with every other cell on the board. And the outcomes which emerge at the aggregate level are very difficult to predict in the short term, while at the same time having a degree of longer-run structure.

This game can be adapted to think about economic growth, and the behaviour of the individual ants, or companies, which generate growth. In this case, each cell can be thought of as being occupied by a firm offering a particular set of products in a particular position in the market(s) in which it operates. The relative heights of the firms in various cells on the board correspond, fairly obviously, to their relative economic size.

The game can be started by all the cells being filled by companies of identical size, each producing a fairly low level of output. This is an approximate description of the capitalist economies at an early stage of their development, in the first half of the nineteenth century. Even then, of course, some firms were larger than others, but the massive conglomerates which have characterized the last one hundred years had not really emerged. So the assumption that companies start off all at the same size in the opening decades of the capitalist game is not an unreasonable one to make.

Figure 12.1 illustrates just such a starting point. The board is a 15 by 15 square, making 225 cells in all. So in this example there are 225 firms to begin with. There is no special significance attached to this particular number, and the game could equally well be played with either fewer or more cells. With a very large number, however, practical difficulties of computation start to arise (certainly on a PC), while with a small number, some of the diversity of actual economies may be lost.

If we think of the 225 as a sample of firms in real life, it should give us a reasonable picture of what is going on amongst the much larger population of firms which actually exists. As it happens, the same principle was used with the solutions of our theoretical model of ants in Chapter 1. We did not populate it with the enormous number of individual ants which make up real colonies. Instead, we used a more limited number, which eases computational problems and yet is sufficiently large to provide a reasonable sample of how a much larger population would behave.

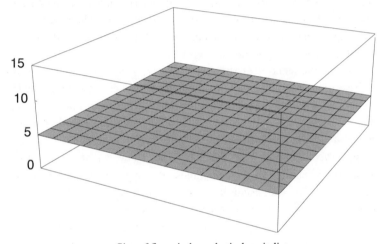

FIGURE 12.1 Size of firms in hypothetical capitalist economy:
early phase of development, c. 1870

The value of the output of each firm is measured on the vertical axis. The amount which each firm is assumed to produce at the start is arbitrarily set at 5. There is no significance whatsoever in this figure. But in order to make comparisons both over time during the same game and between the outcomes of a series of different plays of the game, there has to be a benchmark at which to start. The overall size of the economy at any point in time can be measured in a very straightforward way by adding together the sizes – the heights – of the individual cells. So in Figure 12.1, the total value of output in our hypothetical economy is 225 x 5, equals 1,125 (which the reader can interpret as millions or billions of dollars, pounds or whatever, if he or she so chooses).

The sizes of the firms occupying each individual cell evolve over time according to a few simple rules. The principle of positive feedback, of the intensification of impacts, is an integral part of our model, or, as we have been thinking about it so far, the rules of the game. A firm's rate of growth – the speed at which its height changes in Figure 12.1 – depends on two factors. First, a set of rules, as yet unspecified, about how it reacts to changes which arise in our model. Second, its existing size. But the two are connected explicitly: the impact of any given change will be bigger, the larger the firm already is. So positive changes will feed on themselves and lead the firm to become even bigger, and negative ones will drive it even further in the opposite direction.

The most important of the rules connects each individual cell with every other cell on the board, to decide the influence of changes in the size of a firm on every other company. Many of these connections are very weak, for the actions of any individual company do not have much of a discernible impact on many firms in the economy.

But other connections are much stronger. Some of these are positive. This may be because of the complimentary nature of their products, so that, say, a tyre manufacturer or oil company will benefit if the car industry prospers. Or we can think of firms being linked in strategic alliances, as in the airline industry, so that the growth of one firm can benefit the other. But some connections between firms are negative, representing firms which directly compete with each other, where the gains of one are often directly at the expense of the other.

An extension of this rule involves connecting each particular firm, not just with all the other firms to varying degrees, but to itself. This enhances the principle of increasing returns introduced above. A positive link from a cell back on to itself means that if growth takes place on this particular cell from elsewhere in the network, the effect will be enhanced. Such links need not be positive. Some parts of the economy operate under diminishing returns, and so a negative connection is appropriate in these circumstances. Ideally, some of these self-connections could vary from positive to negative, implying increasing returns over an initial size of the firm, followed by a move to diminishing ones. But in the first instance, the model is deliberately kept as simple and as straightforward as possible.

Finally, a rule is introduced to reflect the activity of mergers and acquisitions. An easy way to do this is to allow a firm's activities to spill over, as it were, into activities which are very close to its existing ones. So growth in the cells immediately around a cell is positively related to the size of that particular cell. Of course, mergers or acquisitions can be between companies which produce quite different things. But this rule is a simple way of introducing the principle of merger and acquisition activity. It is by no means ideal, but the main interest of the model is to see how the interconnections between firms discussed above, combined with the basic rule on increasing returns, affect the overall rate of economic activity in the model.

There is no doubt that these rules could be refined, added to, and made more complicated. But the purpose of the exercise is to show how readily a model based on individual ants, or firms in this case, acting according to a small number of simple rules, can be constructed. And it does give a reasonable representation of the key features of the process of economic growth over the past one hundred years or so.

Each of the ants, or firms, in this model is connected to every other firm. Before we can play the game, however, we need to decide the strengths of the links. Once this is done, each individual agent has its *own* set of rules which govern its growth and evolution over time.

This diversity between agents is an important principle of the real world. Firms *are* different, and it is very hard to transfer directly the qualities which make any particular firm successful to another company. At one level, for example, Coca Cola is just a firm which makes a sweet, fizzy soft drink. But if that were a complete description, competitors could easily replicate the entire operation. Instead, the company has maintained a dominant position in its market for many decades. The quality of its product may be one reason for this. Yet it is hard to imagine that it is so much better than the products of actual or potential rivals that it can account for Coca Cola's success. The company must be doing lots of other things right.

One way of choosing the strengths of the various links would be to try to use our knowledge of actual connections in an economy to decide their sign and size. But this would require an immense amount of detailed information which would be extremely difficult to acquire. A much more straightforward method is to select them at random. By using an appropriate way of doing this,* we can ensure that many of the links are weak, while some smaller proportions are strong and positive, and some are strong and negative.

This is far more sensible than it may at first appear, for it offers a fairly powerful test of the realism of the whole approach. As we saw in Chapter 10, the growth rates of the Western economies over long periods of time are remarkably similar. After allowing for inflation, national income per head in the United States, France and Germany has grown at just under 2 per cent a year over the past century or so. The weakest performers over this period, such as the UK, have still grown at 1.5 per cent a year. And with the exception of Japan, no country has managed to grow by more than 2.5 per cent a year. Despite the fact that the historical experiences, the institutional structures and the balance between various types of economic activity within each country are all different, the overall growth rates averaged over long periods of time are very much the same. This suggests very strongly that it is the general principles upon which these economies are based, rather than any set of circumstances particular to any one of them, which accounts for their performance over time.

Our model of growth is certainly based upon general principles, rather than on knowledge of how any particular economy operates in practice. And each set of connections in the model, chosen at random, can be thought of as a separate country, with its own institutions and sectors. So we can readily form a large number of artificial economies, each of which is different to the others, exactly as in reality.

Between 1870 and 1997 American income per head grew by a factor of around ten, which is typical of the Western economies as a whole. So we can allow each of our hypothetical economies to evolve until the average level of economic activity across all of them has risen by a similar amount. The spread of growth rates generated in these economies can then be compared. If the simple rules of behaviour in our model offer a realistic

---

* For example, by drawing from a normal distribution with mean zero.

description of the principles on which capitalist economies operate, we would expect a spread of growth rates to emerge which is similar to that of the actual Western economies.*

But before discussing the tests of the model and how it performs when compared to the real world, it is interesting to follow the evolution of a single artificial economy over time. This exercise, it must be stressed, is for illustrative purposes, and no claim is being made that the figures below represent precisely what has happened to, say, the US economy over various periods of time. Rather, they are indicative of the type of evolution which capitalist economies follow. Thinking back to Chapters 8 and 9, when we discussed both conventional economic models of the business cycle and our ants-based version, no single solution of the theoretical models was expected to correspond to the precise behaviour of the American economy. The models were judged by comparing regularities which emerged when they were solved repeatedly with the properties of the actual data. Exactly the same principle is at work here, and the figures below show, for interest, a single solution of our model.

The economy plotted in Figure 12.1 is an approximation of a capitalist economy of the mid-nineteenth century, with many rather small firms, and a low level of overall output. Figure 12.2 shows the structure of one of these artificial economies when its total output has doubled in size. In terms of income per head,† this corresponds to the United States $c.1910$, assuming the starting point of 1870 for Figure 12.1.

The landscape is distinctly rugged. In Figure 12.1, each individual firm was assumed to produce a level of output of 5. Yet in Figure 12.2, by reading across from the tops of the highest peaks to the vertical axis, we can see that some firms are producing a level of output of some 12 or 13, while others remain sunk in the depths, at much lower levels of output.

---

* External trade does not enter explicitly into the models. But this does not imply that it is absent. The principle of increasing returns to some individual companies in the models could arise, for example, precisely because of the advantages which size confers when operating in export markets.
† In the simulated economies, population is assumed to be constant. Population growth could easily be factored in, but our interest is in comparing the evolution of per capita income in the real world with those of our artificial economies.

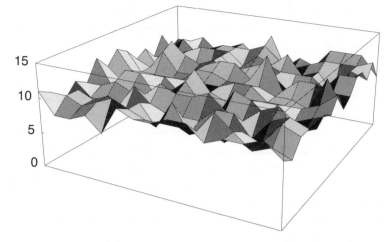

FIGURE 12.2 Size of firms in hypothetical capitalist economy: c. 1910

Figure 12.3 plots the outcome for the hypothetical economy when output has increased five times from its starting point. In per capita terms, again starting as it were in 1870, America reached this level around 1960.

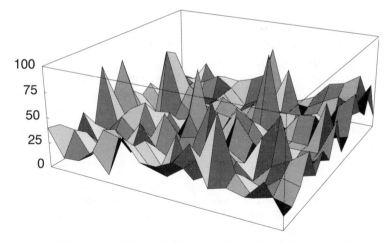

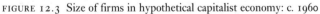

FIGURE 12.3 Size of firms in hypothetical capitalist economy: c. 1960

In this chart, the diversity which opens up between the sizes of the various firms begins to look much clearer. Peering closely into the hollows, we can see that the heights of some of the individual cells remain very low, scarcely higher than in Figure 12.1. In contrast, some have grown dramatically, with the biggest showing an increase over the starting levels of almost twenty-fold. Finally, Figure 12.4 shows the illustrative outcome in this particular hypothetical economy in the late 1990s, when per capita income has grown around ten times from its starting values.

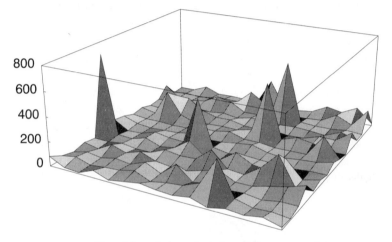

FIGURE 12.4 Size of firms in hypothetical capitalist economy: late 1990s

The structure of the chart appears to be much smoother, but this is quite deceptive. Compared to Figure 12.3, the overall level of output has only doubled, but a small number of firms have now become very large indeed. The two largest spikes in the chart correspond to output levels around seven times higher than the biggest in Figure 12.3.

Again, it must be emphasized that these charts simply illustrate the evolution over time of a single artificial economy operating according to our rules. But the distribution of firm sizes which emerges in Figure 12.4 is entirely typical of such examples. And, much more importantly, it is *qualitatively* similar to the distribution which we observe in reality. Recall that in the *Fortune* 500, the top ten companies in America have total sales somewhat greater than the combined sales of those ranked in positions

101 to 200. In our model, we only have 225 companies in total. The sales of the top three are slightly larger than those in positions 26 to 50. And this same sort of principle applies as we move down the rankings. In the *Fortune* list, the sales of the top 100 put together are distinctly larger than those ranked between 101 and 500 in size, and in Figure 12.4 the output of the top fifty firms is also much bigger than those from 51st to 225th in size.

By creating many different economies, each with its own connections between firms and hence with its own history, we can observe the spread of outcomes of average annual growth rates which our model generates. In each of these artificial economies, the principles of how firms are linked together are exactly the same. We can think of them, in other words, as all playing the same game called capitalism. The structure of each economy allows economic activity to flourish. But the strengths of the various connections between the firms are different in each economy.

Figure 12.5 plots the spread of growth rates for 250 solutions of our model, 250 hypothetical countries, in which total output rises on average by a factor of ten, the same amount as in the actual Western economies between 1870 and the late 1990s.

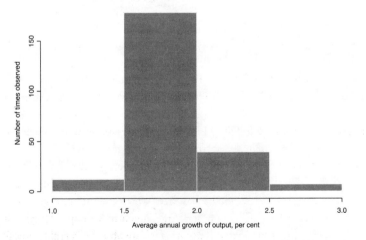

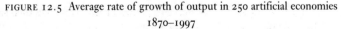

FIGURE 12.5 Average rate of growth of output in 250 artificial economies
1870–1997

The clear majority of cases are concentrated in the 1.5 to 2 per cent annual rate of growth. This is very similar to the actual experience of seventeen capitalist economies, whose real per capita output growth is summarized in Figure 12.6.

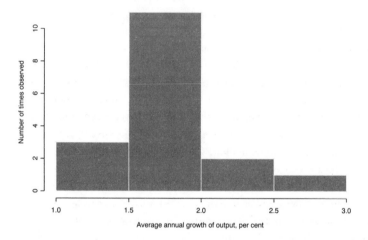

FIGURE 12.6 Average rate of growth of output in 17 capitalist economies 1870–1997

The range of growth rates observed in Figures 12.5 and 12.6 are very similar. The outcomes of the model lead to a smaller proportion of countries in the 1 to 1.5 per cent band than is the case in reality, but overall Figure 12.5 gives a reasonable approximation to what actually happened.

The hypothetical economies in Figure 12.5 are all part of the capitalist growth club, achieving sustained but slow growth which leads to massive expansion over a century or so. The exercise can be repeated for another group of economies who all start off much poorer. Specifically, 250 artificial economies were created using exactly the same principles as above, except that the average output level was set in each of them at only 40 per cent of that of the capitalist club economies. In 1870, this was the average per head of the Latin American economies compared to those of Western Europe.

Over the same time period as the capitalist club economies, the poor countries grew more slowly, so that in these simulations, by the mid-1990s, the average level of output had fallen to only 30 per cent of that of the richer group. Again, this is very much in line with what actually happened.

The very simple model of economic growth set out in this chapter is based, as with our ants, on individual agents – companies in this case – and the connections between them. A small number of straightforward rules are used to describe these links. The principles upon which each company operates are the same, but the exact strength of the various connections varies from company to company, so that each agent is unique. This diversity is a fundamental feature of the real world. A further crucial aspect of reality captured in our model is that the feedbacks to economic activities are not restricted, as in orthodox economics, to diminishing or constant returns to scale, but also embrace increasing returns.

Despite the very basic nature of the model, it describes key aspects of long-term economic growth rather well. At the micro-level, the distribution of the sizes of individual firms which emerges is similar to that observed in the real world. At the aggregate level, the spread of growth rates between different members of the same economic club – countries which start off with similar levels of output per head – coincides closely with what has actually happened over the past century or so. And the disparities between rich and poor clubs become larger, not smaller, over time, exactly as in reality, and in direct contrast to the predictions of orthodox models of economic growth.

Once again, the principles of our model of ant behaviour point the way forward to a better understanding of an important economic problem. The approach described above has no pretence to provide *the* answer to the question of long-term economic growth, but it gives a better description of reality than does orthodox economics.

Conclusion: Less Can Be More

Karl Marx once famously wrote 'Philosophers have sought to interpret the world. The point, however, is to change it.' He was completely wrong. Politicians have sought to change the world. But the point is to interpret it correctly.

Liberal intellectuals often feel intuitively uncomfortable with the whole idea that social and economic questions are capable of being modelled and analysed in a systematic way. James Buchan expresses this view in a straightforward way in his fascinating book *Frozen Desire*: 'a market cannot operate by laws, for the laws would be discovered, and it would cease to be a market.' But the unease arises for a variety of less obvious reasons, from a feeling that the concept of free will is undermined, to the view that humans are too complicated for their behaviour to be represented in this way. Perhaps most important is the attitude that modelling human systems in this way implies that they, and by implication the individuals of which they are comprised, can be controlled.

Many of these fears are assuaged by the complex systems approach. Insights into a wide range of social and economic issues can be given by models built on the premise that individuals behave as if they followed simple guidelines, rules of thumb appropriate to the specific context. The key point here is that even if individual rules of behaviour are known exactly, the resulting behaviour of the system still cannot be predicted and controlled in a precise manner.

In my model of the business cycle in Chapter 9, for example, individual firms follow very simple rules which can be written down in a couple of lines of maths. But the cycles which emerge in the overall economy through companies following these rules are subtle, just as actual business cycles are, and are not susceptible to prediction and control. As in the basic model of our ants, the rules have a probabilistic as well as a deterministic component. Understanding laws of behaviour, particularly probabilistic ones, means neither that the laws are thereby eliminated, nor that individuals are automatically open to the tyranny of control.

Generations of policy-makers have been raised in the mechanistic view of the world, with the checklist mentality: to achieve a particular set of aims, draw up a list of policies and simply tick them off. It is a comforting environment in which to live, being seemingly dependable, predictable and controllable. The planners of the Soviet Union believed this to be the case. But their economy ultimately could not compete with the more disordered world of capitalism, not as it is portrayed in conventional economics, but as it actually exists.

The complex systems approach makes life more difficult, not just for policy-makers but for scholars and businessmen alike. Unfortunately, the world cannot be changed to suit our convenience. Students of Ancient Greek would no doubt be very appreciative if all the verbs in that language could be changed to make them well-behaved, for almost every single one contains some degree of irregularity in its conjugation. But this simply cannot be done.

The inability to control the economy or society in a precise way in the short term does not mean in any way that the actions of governments have no effects. They most certainly do. But conventional thinking offers an account of such impacts which is at best incomplete and at worst positively misleading. The effect of any given set of measures can vary substantially, depending upon the particular circumstances in which they are introduced. Quite frequently, small changes will have only small consequences, just as common sense suggests they should. But, unfortunately, common sense may not always be a very good guide. Common sense, after all, indicates that the sun goes round the Earth, for we can see it move across the sky and the Earth appears to stay still. Sometimes, a change of identical magnitude which in a different context only had a small impact will now have a large effect, and occasionally it will have a really dramatic one. A subtle approach is needed to try to approximate this complex reality.

Despite the difficulties involved in managing a complex world, governments still have an important role to play. They should do very much less in terms of detailed, short-term intervention. And they should spend much more time thinking about the overall framework of whatever particular problem is at issue. For it is here that governments have the potential to achieve a great deal. Less can be more.

The outcome of the basic ants model – the proportion of the colony visiting one of the food sites – is unpredictable and uncontrollable in the short term. But, over a long period of time, the structure of that outcome is open to influence. For example, Figures 1.2 and 1.3 illustrate quite different distributions for the amounts of time which the colony spends at either extreme, when the proportion visiting one of the sites is close to either zero or 100 per cent. If the ants have only a low propensity to switch behaviour, the colony is close to the extremes for a large part of the time, whilst if the propensity is high, a more even split between the two food sources occupies much of the time.

If the propensity of ants to switch behaviour could be altered, a dramatic influence would be exerted on the overall behaviour of the colony. If the desired outcome were one of a more even distribution between the two food sites, the policy-maker should focus attention on trying to make ants more likely to change their behaviour. The impact of this in the short term remains unpredictable. The colony could never be prevented from spending *some* of its time close to the two extremes, but the amount of such time could be reduced enormously.

The gains from being able to alter the distribution of outcomes in the ants experiment itself – however that might be achieved – are of little consequence to the rest of us. But in areas where the ants model illuminates human behaviour, they can be considerable. An important direct application of the ants model, which we saw in Chapter 2, was to the world of foreign exchange, with dealers on the trading floors being cast in the role of ants.

The foreign exchange markets offer irresistible temptations to governments to intervene, often with damaging consequences for their economies. Over a very long period of time, the average value of one currency against another will be determined by economic fundamentals, and in particular by their relative rates of inflation. If one country experiences a zero rate of inflation and another one of 4 per cent, say, over the course of two or three decades the exchange will adjust to reflect this. But at any point in time, the value of a currency may deviate substantially from the rate indicated by fundamentals. And these deviations, whether above or below such a rate, can persist for long periods.

Governments may well want to reduce the amount of time which currencies spend being substantially over- or under-valued, when there are large deviations away from the rates indicated by economic fundamentals. But there are no realistic, predictable short-term relationships between changes in the various policy instruments available to governments and changes in the exchange rate. During the first half of 1998, for example, sterling has been strong against other European currencies. This is widely attributed to the higher interest rates which now exist in the UK. Yet in 1992, for example, British interest rates were even higher. These culminated not in a strong currency but in the summary devaluation and ejection of sterling from the European Exchange Rate mechanism, delivering a blow to the domestic credibility of the then Conservative government from which it did not recover even by the time of the 1997 election.

The ants model shows that if foreign exchange dealers do not change their minds very frequently, the system will spend a very large proportion of its time at the extremes. Once a currency becomes under- or over-valued, it is very likely to remain there for a long period of time. But if individuals have a high propensity to alter their behaviour, such persistence is much less likely. Governments can never prevent periods of substantial currency over-valuation, for example, from taking place, but by encouraging rather than restraining speculative behaviour, they can help to ensure that these are much shorter than they otherwise would be. Speculation, often portrayed as the enemy of governments, can be stimulated to achieve desirable ends.

The basic ants model is, of course, just one variant of the overall complex systems approach which I propose in this book. Crime and family structures are typical of another set of such models which describe a wide range of social and economic questions. These are characterized by what can be termed different regimes. In the simple models set out in Chapters 3 and 4, for example, there is a path along which crime is high and one on which it is low, and similarly in the case of families, for the proportion of the population which is married. Switches between these regimes are often both abrupt and dramatic.

The real challenge for governments is to try to ensure that society moves, for example, on the low rather than the high crime path. This is not a matter of detailed, short-term interventions and targets, but of creating the right overall environment. Deciding how to bring this about is not by any means a trivial task, whereas any charlatan can draw up a conventional policy checklist in the course of an afternoon. But the potential gains from success in the former are far greater than anything which can be achieved by the latter.

There are a number of important questions in which the key issue is not the precise position of the economy within any particular regime, but the nature of the regime itself. Governments do have the power to influence this decisively, both for better and for worse. A striking example of success in setting the right environment is the American Marshall Plan for Europe in the aftermath of the Second World War. European governments faced many problems, but the key decision was whether to retain planning as the basis for the economy or to move back to a more liberal, market-oriented system. Strong domestic support existed throughout Europe for the former option, particularly in France and Italy where Communist Parties were very powerful. But a precondition of receipt of Marshall Aid, which in itself was not an absolutely enormous amount of money, was that governments should relax plans and controls and move back towards the market economy. The state still had an important role to play, but it was no longer the sole arbiter of many economic decisions. Encouraging Europeans to follow this path was the single most decisive feature of the Marshall Plan.

Inflation is another issue which can be characterized as falling broadly into a small number of distinct regimes, as discussed at the end of Chapter 7. During times of serious civil disturbances, such as in civil wars or in the immediate aftermath of major wars, inflation can soar to astronomical rates. On a much less dramatic scale, the antagonism between capital and labour was a key reason for the surge in inflation in many European countries in the mid-1970s. But in general, capitalist economies tend to deliver rates of inflation which average close to zero.

In the current circumstances, the attitude of the American authorities is very sensible. The monetary authorities – the Federal Reserve – are charged with achieving broad price stability and, interpreting this somewhat liberally to encompass small, positive rates of inflation, they carry out this task successfully without inflicting damage on the productive sector of the economy. They have done so by taking a broad perspective on inflation, and deciding that there is no serious, structural threat to the present low-inflation regime. Inflation will move up and down over the course of the business cycle in an erratic way, but in itself this is not a matter of concern. The key question to decide is the overall perspective on inflation, whether it is likely to be on average low over the course of a number of years. If the answer is 'yes', monetary policy can be on average fairly relaxed. And there is no need for the authorities to intervene at the slightest sign of a cyclical rise in inflation.

In contrast, most European governments, and the new European Central Bank, are obsessed with achieving far more precise, short-term inflation targets. This requires far more frequent, active intervention by the monetary authorities. Such an approach is at best foolish and at worst positively harmful. It is simply not possible to predict inflation with sufficient accuracy to know what the appropriate form of intervention should be at any point in time.

In much of Europe, the neurosis of precise inflation targeting in the past ten to fifteen years has led to tight monetary conditions and to real rates of interest which are historically very high. These in turn have – not surprisingly – dampened the long-term buoyancy of business expecta-tions, leading growth to be below its potential rate, and as a result insufficient jobs are being created to reduce unemployment. Govern-ments should accept that inflation does move up and down over the business cycle, but provided that the conditions for a low inflation regime overall remain in place, this is nothing to worry about. Attempts to intervene and hit precise targets do more harm than good.

Intervention to try to control the movements of the business cycle are similarly misplaced. Again, as is documented in Chapter 6, it is simply not possible to forecast with sufficient precision the state of the economy in, say, one year's time in order to know what measures to take now to bring about a different outcome – even if the impact of measures such as changes in taxation or public expenditure were known with sufficient accuracy, which they are not.

In this instance, governments need to accept that the business cycle can never be abolished, but is an inherent feature of market economies. Decisions are taken by individual agents operating under uncertainty, and it is this which is the cause of the permanence of the business cycle. The role of governments should be confined to trying to mitigate the consequences of the cycle rather than to try to smooth it out or eliminate it.

A particularly important aspect of this is unemployment. Unemployment fluctuates in a fairly regular way with the course of the business cycle, falling during booms and rising during slumps. Every so often a very sharp recession takes place which leads to a large increase in unemployment, of which the mid-1970s and early 1980s are the two most recent examples. This need not be a major concern. In the United States, for example, unemployment rose from under 5 per cent in 1973 to over 8 per cent in 1975. Yet as the economy recovered during the next upswing of the cycle, unemployment fell to under 6 per cent. Similarly, it rose to 9.5 per cent in 1982, and was back down to around 5 per cent by 1988. The relationship between economic growth and unemployment over the course of the business cycle was not disrupted. In the UK in the mid-1970s, unemployment rose from 3 per cent in 1973 to nearly 6 per cent in 1976. But this was entirely consistent with the sharp slow-down in economic growth which took place.

The problem really arises when unemployment moves onto a different, higher path, when a recession precipitates an increase which is much greater than expected given the size of the economic slow-down. In Germany, for example, unemployment more than trebled from under 1 per cent in 1973 to well over 3 per cent in 1975, and again from 3 per cent in 1980 to almost 8 per cent in 1983. In each case, the rise was approximately double that which was warranted by the depth of the two recessions.

In such circumstances, a particularly large stock of unemployment is created, which subsequent economic recoveries find difficult to remove. Conventional economic theory does not admit the long-term persistence of unemployment, of an imbalance between the supply of and demand for labour, unless there are obstacles to the workings of the price mechanism which is assumed to work to clear all markets. Hence we see the emphasis in policy on labour market 'flexibility', of the need for real wages to fall, and for the welfare state and its benefits to be cut. As it happens, there is an alternative explanation for the persistence of high European unemployment, mentioned above in the context of inflation – that growth has been inadequate over the course of several business cycles because of tight monetary policy and the fixation with short-term inflation targeting.

But these are arguments about what to do once an unusually high level of unemployment has been created, once unemployment has been placed onto a higher path. Governments can never know in advance either the scale of a recession or whether it will lead to an unexpectedly high increase in unemployment. But when the economy has actually begun to slow down sharply – when a deep recession is beginning to be a matter of fact rather than one of prediction – measures should be brought in very quickly which reduce the possibility of a particularly massive loss of jobs taking place. Such policies could only be temporary. Further, there will inevitably be a degree of waste involved in widespread job subsidies. But once jobs have been destroyed on a large scale, it seems very difficult to generate the environment in which they can be created again. Unemployment can be placed on a high path which may persist for decades. It is more effective to try to head off the possibility of massive and rapid job loss, and then to wait for the natural upturn in the economy to reduce unemployment once again.

The world of business has a much better intuitive understanding of the complexity of the world than government does, and certainly than most academic economists. Business people realize that it is futile to search for *the* best plan, for the future is to a large extent inherently unpredictable. Their task is to come up with good plans which offer reasonable prospects of success. Of course, short-term plans and targets exist. But the crucial role of the board of any successful company is to think strategically, to think about the overall environment in which the firm operates. Anticipating, adapting to and even trying to influence changes in the longer-term structure is the real key to success.

An important indicator of success for many companies, particularly those involved in consumer markets, is how they perform in terms of market share against a small number of major competitors. It is easy to secure temporary advantage by, say, a price promotion or a large increase in advertising expenditure. Such tactics do have their place, but the real challenge is to understand the wider environment, the broader potential for a brand, not just how to manage it in the face of competition, but how it fits into the portfolio of the company itself.

Companies should not place too much emphasis on the state of the overall business cycle and, by and large, they do not. Even the largest company in the world, General Motors, is more damaged by the loss of one percentage point of market share to a major rival than it is to a downturn in the US economy. The main focus should be on competitors and the long-term strategy to adopt. Of course, the immediacy of a boom or slump affects companies, but these come and go, whereas rivals who steal a strategic march can inflict permanent damage.

A wealth of evidence on success and failure in companies is provided in the magnum opus of Alfred Chandler of the Harvard Business School. Entitled *Scale and Scope of Industrial Capitalism*, the book examines the detailed histories of the 200 largest manufacturing companies in the three leading industrial nations, America, Britain and Germany, in the latter part of the nineteenth and first part of the twentieth centuries when the foundations of global capitalism and large firms were laid. An absolute prerequisite of success was the ability of the company management to define a suitable set of long-term goals for the organization.* This is not in itself a guarantee of success, but a failure to carry out this task is a recipe for potential disaster. A crucial aspect of clear goal setting is that everyone in the company then knows the sort of behaviour which is likely to lead to approval. In this way, innovation and commitment at all levels is encouraged.

In many ways, complex systems analysis formalizes what successful business people know instinctively. But there are several implications which are worth mentioning. Once we admit the possibility that individual tastes and behaviour can be influenced directly by those of others, gaining a lead on rivals can create a virtuous circle in which the market position of a company or brand becomes stronger simply because it is already seen to be popular. So it is important not just to innovate but to test such developments in the marketplace as early as possible. A new product may seize the imagination and rapidly build up a powerful

---

* Chandler gives the example of a British company in which the board spent most of its time doing cost-accounting in longhand. Even the use of a slide rule was frowned upon. It did not prosper.

position, while if it is endlessly tested and refined within the confines of the firm, rival companies may themselves introduce concepts which pre-empt its potential success.

The self-reinforcing nature of success rarely means that a company thereby gains complete dominance over its competitors. The simple reason for this is that it is usually quite easy for customers to change their minds – indeed, switching opinions or behaviour is the whole essence of the basic ants model. In the case, say, of the appropriate choice of techniques to be used in nuclear power plants, the successful technology can certainly gain 100 per cent market share. The investment is extremely expensive and very long-lived. Once the plant has been built, it is not really feasible to pull it down and construct one of a different kind. With a bar of chocolate, in contrast, consumers can experiment with rival brands at minimal expense. Buying a particular brand today does not preclude the purchase of a competing one tomorrow. The principles of positive feedback, of the reinforcement of the position of dominant brands, still apply. Popular products sustain their popularity in part simply because they are popular. But, except in the case of extremely expensive purchases, this mechanism does not lead to the elimination of rivals and permanent market control.

Orthodox economics is a not a completely empty box, and my arguments do not involve its complete rejection but rather an extension, a generalization which takes into account, unlike conventional theory, the fundamental fact that people are influenced directly by the behaviour of others. The challenge of providing a tolerable description of a complex world with interacting agents is certainly hard. This may have been the basis behind the great physicist Max Planck's alleged remark in the 1930s to the leading economist John Maynard Keynes. The mathematics which is actually used in most of economics, not just then but even now, was perfectly straightforward and even trivial to a man with Planck's background. But when Keynes asked him whether he had ever thought of taking up economics, Planck thought for a moment. 'No,' he replied, 'the maths is too hard.' Yet the gains from a better understanding of how the economy and society operate are potentially enormous.

For too long, the social sciences have been divided into the hard, represented by economics with its mathematical rigour, and the soft, such as criminology or sociology, where more verbal reasoning and skills are displayed. This split would have been incomprehensible to the great founding fathers of economics, such as Adam Smith, who regarded themselves first and foremost as political economists. They were driven to understand the world in order to create opportunities for making it a better place, and used evidence from a wide variety of sources to support their theoretical arguments. By no means everything which they wrote has stood the test of time. But their most important contribution was to begin the process of trying to understand society and the economy by systematic thinking. They were concerned, ultimately, with trying to interpret the world correctly.

Can conventional economic forecasting ever be successful? Some possible defences -- but still guilty as charged!

This appendix takes up the points raised in the footnotes on pages 87 and 90. The arguments are in part too complicated to put in the main text, and in addition they rather disrupt the flow. Nevertheless, they need to be discussed.

Footnote, p. 87, Chapter 6

Most forecasts of, say, GDP growth or inflation are published for the next year rather than for the next quarter. On this basis, the data looks more regular and appears to have more structure. Figure App.1 plots quarterly changes in American national output over the post-war period, and Figure App.2 plots annual changes, on a quarter-by-quarter basis.

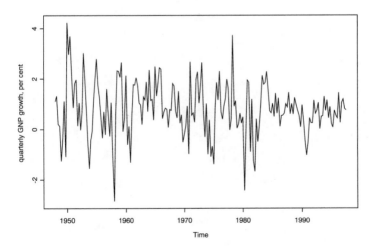

FIGURE APP.1 Quarterly growth rate of US real GNP 1948–97

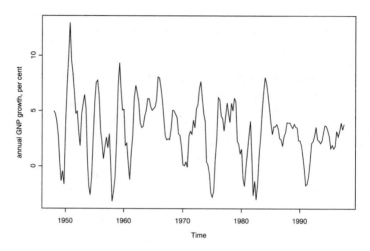

FIGURE APP.2 Annual growth rate of US real GNP 1948–97

The annual growth series appears to move up and down more smoothly, with less of the very short-term irregularities which characterize the quarterly series. This is apparently confirmed when we plot the annual data in three-dimensional form in Figure App.3 in the same way the quarterly data was plotted in Figure 6.7 on p. 89.

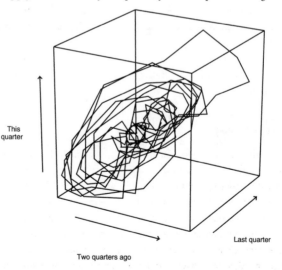
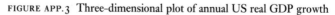

FIGURE APP.3 Three-dimensional plot of annual US real GDP growth

This seems to have far more structure and pattern to its behaviour than does the quarterly data, with a far more obvious cyclical pattern as it traces out loops in the three-dimensional plot. But this is simply an illusion of arithmetic. We cannot use this structure to improve the accuracy of forecasts of American GNP growth. Suppose we denote the GNP series by the symbol y. Then y(t) is GNP at any particular time – the third quarter of 1955, the second quarter of 1986, or whenever. The change from quarter to quarter is $y(t) - y$ at time $t - 1$, i.e. $y(t) - y(t - 1)$

In the same way we can write the annual change as y at time t minus y four time periods ago – in other words, four quarters previously: $y(t) - y(t - 4)$.

But we can write this last term in a different way, which simply says that the change over the course of a year is the sum of the changes over the individual quarters:

$$y(t) - y(t - 4) = [y(t) - y(t - 1)] + [y(t - 1) - y(t - 2)] + [y(t - 2) - y(t - 3)] + [y(t - 3) - y(t - 4)]$$

If we remove the square brackets and collect terms, we see that $y(t - 1)$, $y(t - 2)$ and $y(t - 3)$ drop out from the right-hand side of the expression.

Suppose now that we are at the end of period $(t - 1)$, or at the start of t, whichever way we choose to look at it, and want to forecast $y(t) - y(t - 4)$. We already know what has happened to $y(t - 1)$, $y(t - 2)$, $y(t - 3)$ and $y(t - 4)$. So the task reduces itself to forecasting $[y(t) - y(t - 1)]$ – in other words, the quarterly growth of GNP in the next quarter. And if we want to forecast a year ahead, the task, in the same way, is equivalent to forecasting each of the next four quarters on a quarterly basis. The annual series simply look more regular because, when we are trying to forecast it in the next *quarter* at any point in time, we already know what has happened to three-quarters of it. But we do not know this if we want to forecast a year ahead.

Footnote, p. 90, Chapter 6

Those engaged with the orthodox business of modelling and forecasting the economy – using the word 'business' advisedly, for in Europe at least such activities are usually underwritten by large grants and subsidies from the taxpayer – do try to offer what they regard as a more subtle defence of their activities. One aspect of this is to argue that the criticism that the data lacks sufficient structure for their activities to be meaningful misrepresents what they are trying to achieve. The few econometricians who are aware of non-linear signal processing techniques imagine that they have a defence against the apparently powerful evidence of the three-dimensional charts in Chapter 6. In each of our equations, econometricians argue, the movements of the variable which we are trying to explain – such as consumer spending – depend upon a number of entirely separate factors.

In the jargon, these individual equations are known as 'multi-variate', for the simple reason that they contain more than one variable. The three-dimensional charts make no allowance for this, because the structure of the data is only investigated using its own past history, and not the history of other factors which might influence it. To use another technical term, this is a 'uni-variate' representation of the data, because only one variable is involved.

At first glance, this might appear to be a powerful charge. Charts such as Figures 6.6 and 6.7 do plot the data purely in terms of its value now and its value in previous periods. But a moment's reflection is sufficient for us to appreciate that this is exactly the way in which the evidence should be presented, regardless of how many variables may influence the series.

Imagine an old-fashioned horror story, in which our gentleman hero is summoned into the rural wilderness to investigate a gruesome series of murders. The perpetrator, in true melodramatic tradition, only strikes on the night when the moon is full. Our sleuth sits and ponders when the next assault will take place. In a flash of inspiration, he connects the times of the crimes with the date of the full moon, and so is able to predict correctly the next outrage. We might entitle our story *The Intrepid Econometrician*, for our protagonist has built a successful multi-variate model. The movements in one variable – the dates of the murders – have been connected with those of another – the dates of the full moon.

But our man could have been of an altogether more pedantic frame of mind. He may simply have noted that there was a regular interval between one murder and the next, and extrapolated from that. It would spoil the drama, but this uni-variate model, which accounts for the times of the murders purely on the basis of their own past history, would be just as effective at predicting the time of the next murder as the more sinister multi-variate model connecting them to the full moon.

By definition, in this novelette the times of the murders are determined by the dates of the full moon. But it is precisely the regularity of the movements of this variable which give structure to the patterns observed in the dates of the murders. In these circumstances, successful predictions can be made by both multi- and uni-variate techniques. The former tell a much more interesting story, but both are equally effective at prediction.

A more intelligent monster would commit his foul deeds, not with regularity, but at random. He might, for example, shake a dice every day and decide to kill someone if and only if a six appeared. If our fiend noted the outcomes of the rolls of the dice in his diary, a clever econometrician who gained access to this data could discover a match between the dates of the murders and the number six being shaken.

A perfect multi-variate model would have been built, accounting successfully for the entire previous history of the murders. But this would be useless for prediction, because the outcome of the roll of a dice is a random event. Neither multi- nor uni-variate techniques would be of any use for forecasting. The data series for the dates of the murders lacks the underlying structure which is required for any sort of reasonable prediction to be made.

The above story deals, in non-technical terms, with states of the world in which the auto-correlation function is reasonably reliable in informing us about the structure underlying any given time series of data. If the data is generated by a strongly non-linear process, this may not be the case. But the word 'strongly' is certainly the operative one here. For example, many standard chaotic series, such as the Lorenz data or the Hénon or cosine maps, reveal structure in their auto-correlation functions, even over a reasonable range of different sampling frequencies. And by definition these series are distinctly non-linear.

The technique of phase space attractor reconstruction *may* fail to reveal structure which exists in particularly exotic, non-linear data. But if this is really the case with the economy, our chances of finding a model which approximates it are, in the current state of scientific knowledge, extremely low. Certainly existing non-linear representations of the quarterly growth of US GNP data account for less than 15 per cent of the total variability of the data, and for UK GDP the figure is below 10 per cent. In other words, existing non-linear models are quite useless for forecasting. Indeed, they can only be described as models in a very loose sense of the word, for the fact that they account for less then 15 per cent of the variability of the data implies that over 85 per cent of the variation which they are trying to explain is left to chance.

This appendix sets out the mathematics of the current fashion in conventional economics, 'real business cycle' theory.

Despite its forbidding nature, the economics are extremely simple. According to RBC theory, cycles do not in fact have an economic explanation, but are caused by random shocks to the system which in turn are caused by technological progress, a factor not explained by the model at all.

The mathematics, while decidedly non-trivial, are linear. This enables the entire economy to be modelled by describing the behaviour of a single 'representative' consumer, for in linear models the whole is just the sum of the parts. Production in this economy is carried out with diminishing returns to both capital and labour, which, as discussed in Chapter 11, rules out economies of scale and positive feedback. And, as discussed in Chapter 8, this approach completely fails to describe the salient features of the post-war American business cycle.

The text below is based on an article by Martin Eichenbaum on real business cycle models in the November 1995 issue of the *Economic Journal*, the UK's leading academic economic journal, which is typical of the whole approach. (Eichenbaum himself, it must be stressed, has been critical of such models.)

Consider the following real business cycle model. The economy is populated by an infinitely lived representative consumer, who ranks alternative streams of consumption and leisure according to the criterion:

$$E_0 \, \beta^t [\ln(C_t) - \vartheta N_t] \qquad (1)$$

Here $0 < \beta < 1$, $\vartheta > 0$, C_t denotes time t consumption, N_t denotes time t hours of work, E_0 denotes the expectations operator conditioned on the time 0 information set.

Time t output, Y_t is produced via the production function

$$Y_t = K_t^{1-\alpha} (N_t X_t)^\alpha \qquad (2)$$

where $0 < \alpha < 1$, K_t denotes the beginning of time t capital stock, and X_t represents the time t level of technology. The stock of capital evolves according to

$$K_{t+1} = (1 - \delta)K_t + I_t \qquad (3)$$

Here I_t denotes time t gross investment and $0 < \delta < 1$. The level of technology evolves according to

$$X_t = X_{t-1}\exp(\gamma + \nu_t) \tag{4}$$

where $\gamma > 0$, ν_t is a serially uncorrelated process with mean 0 and standard deviation σ_ν. The aggregate resource constraint is given by

$$C_t + I_t + G_t \leq Y_t \tag{5}$$

here G_t denotes the time t level of government consumption which evolves according to

$$G_t = X_t\, g_t^* \tag{6}$$

the variable g_t^* is a trend stationary component of government consumption and $g_t = \ln(g_t^*)$ evolves according to

$$g_t = g_0 + g_1 t + \rho\, g_{t-1} + \epsilon_t \tag{7}$$

where g_0 is a constant, $|\rho| < 1$ and ϵ_t is a serially uncorrelated process with mean 0 and standard deviation σ_ϵ.

In the presence of complete markets, the competitive equilibrium of this economy corresponds to the solution of the social planning problem: maximize (1) subject to (2)–(7) by choice of contingency plans for $[C_t, K_{t+1}, N_t, : t \geq 0]$ as a function of the planner's time t information set, which is assumed to include all model variables dated time t and earlier.

This appendix sets out the mathematics of the interacting agent model of business cycles described in Chapter 9.

In terms of symbols, $X_i(t)$ is the growth rate of output of the i'th firm in period t, $Y_i(t)$ is the rate of change of sentiment about the future of the i'th firm formed in period t. The overall rate of growth of output is the (weighted) sum of the individual growth rates, denoted by XBAR(t), and the overall rate of change of sentiment is the (weighted) sum of the individual $Y_i(t)$ variables, shown by YBAR(t).

There are just two equations:

$$X_i(t + 1) = (1 - \alpha)\, X_i(t) + \alpha(\text{YBAR}(t) + \epsilon_i(t)) \qquad (1)$$
$$Y_i(t + 1) = (1 - \beta)\, Y_i(t) - \beta(\text{XBAR}(t) + \eta_i(t)) \qquad (2)$$

where α and β are parameters and $\epsilon_i(t)$ and $\eta_i(t)$ are normally distributed random variables.

This very simple model, in which each agent is different but looks no further ahead than the next period, gives a reasonable description of post-war American business cycle data. There are no external shocks required to generate cycles, the source of which is entirely contained within the model. Cycles exist because of uncertainty about the future, which each firm interprets in a slightly different way. It is particularly important to note the i-subscripts on the $\epsilon(t)$ and $\eta(t)$ variables. In other words, $\epsilon(t)$ and $\eta(t)$ are *not* general shocks to the system at each point in time, but at each point in time each firm makes its *own* draw from the distributions.

The solutions to the equations reported in Chapter 9 are based on the following. The model is populated by 500 individual firms, whose relative sizes are drawn from a distribution based upon the sizes of firms in the *Fortune* 500. The parameters α and β are set, respectively, at 0.80 and 0.25, and ϵ_i and η_i have variances, respectively, of 0.025 and 0.10.

Selected and Annotated Bibliography

I do not attempt in this bibliography to provide an extensive list of references, whether to the current state of and recent developments in conventional economics, or to criticisms of orthodox thinking in the social sciences. It would be easy to document several hundred articles, but this would merely serve to confuse rather than clarify. The aim instead is to provide a selection of references which the interested general reader might wish to follow up.

A literature does now exist on the fundamental concept of the book, that of interacting agents. But this is highly technical and mathematical. A survey is given by Alan Kirman in his chapter in *The Economy as an Evolving Complex System II*, edited by Arthur, Durlauf and Lane on behalf of the Santa Fe Institute and published in the US in 1997 by Addison-Wesley. His original article on ants is in the *Quarterly Journal of Economics*, February 1993, entitled 'Ants, Rationality and Recruitment'. The model introduced by Brian Arthur was published with the Russian mathematicians Yu Ermoliev and Yu Kaniovski in the January–February 1983 issue of *Kibernetica* in their article 'A Generalised Urn Problem and Its Applications'. Even in the context of this technical literature, it is mathematically extremely dense. A slightly less forbidding version is given in his 1989 *Economic Journal* article 'Competing Technologies, Increasing Returns and Lock-in by Historical Events'.

None of the above is really suitable for the non-mathematical reader. For the latter, the description given one hundred years ago of how individual behaviour can be affected by that of others by Thorsten Veblen has not really been bettered. His book, *The Theory of the Leisure Class*, is available in several paperback editions.

Much of the academic empirical work on the behaviour of Western economies only uses data from the 1960s onwards, and lacks a longer-term perspective. The work of Angus Maddison is invaluable in providing such data. His most recent work was published by the OECD in Paris in 1995, and is entitled *Monitoring the World Economy, 1820–1992*.

A more extensive criticism of conventional economics is given in my previous book, *The Death of Economics*, published by Faber and Faber in 1994, which contains its own relevant bibliography. Reference was made to the fact that 'the use of the methodological techniques of the behavioural sciences to test the basic axioms of economic theory is, encouragingly, growing'. This has continued to be the case with important results being both established and confirmed. The article by Graham Loomes in the March 1998 issue of the *Economic Journal* ('Probabilities versus Money: a Test of some Fundamental Assumptions about Rational Decision-Making') is an excellent recent example, and is accessible to the non-mathematical reader.

An enormous literature exists on both crime and the family. Gary Becker's original work on the economic approach to crime appeared in the *Journal of Political Economy* in 1968 ('Crime and Punishment: An Economic Approach'), and a detailed exposition of his thoughts on the family is given in his 1991 book *A Treatise on the Family*, published by Harvard University Press. An extensive recent survey of economic work on crime is set out by Isaac Ehrlich in his article 'Crime, Punishment and the Market for Offences', published in 1996 in the *Journal of Economic Perspectives*.

A technical exposition of the 3-D charts used in chapter 6 is given in my article with Michael Campbell 'Predictability and Economic Time-Series' in *System Dynamics in Economic and Financial Models* edited by Heji, Schumacher, Hanzon and Praagman, published by John Wiley in 1997. Further details of the underlying mathematics are set out in, for example, the 1986 article by Broomhead and King, 'Extracting Qualitative Dynamics from Experimental Data', which appeared in *Physica D*, and Vautard and Ghil's paper 'Singular Spectrum Analysis in Nonlinear Dynamics, with Applications to Paleoclimatic Time Series' in the same journal in 1989.

An extensive set of references to academic work on the business cycle up to the end of the 1980s is provided in A. W. Mullineux's book *Business Cycles and Financial Crises*, published in 1990 by Harvester Wheatsheaf.

The book itself is non-mathematical, though rather densely written. But, with some application, the interested non-economist will find a good discussion of many of the key issues in business cycle theory. More recent discussions of real business cycle theory can be found in the academic journals, such as the articles by Cogley and Nason, 'Output Dynamics in Real Business Cycle Models', in the *American Economic Review* in 1995 and by Rotemberg and Woodford, 'Real Business Cycle Analysis and Forecastability', in the same journal in 1996. A more general and accessible critique is in Paul Krugman's 1994 book *Peddling Prosperity*, published by W. W. Norton. Keynes's own views on the business cycle are set out in chapter 22 of his *General Theory of Employment, Interest and Money*, first published by Macmillans in 1936 and available in more modern editions.

Robert Solow's seminal article on economic growth, 'A Contribution to the theory of Economic Growth', was published in the *Quarterly Journal of Economics* in 1956. An extensive literature exists on so-called 'new growth theory'. A very balanced account is given by Mankiw, Romer and Weil in their article 'A Contribution to the Empirics of Economic Growth' in the *Quarterly Journal of Economics* in 1992.

Index

Taiwan, growth 144
tax incentives 53
taxation xiv, 67, 93, 187
   income tax 76, 93, 96
   increases 92, 94–5
   and marriage 53
   reductions 94, 138
   VAT 93, 95
technological progress 158–9, 165
   and access to information 158–9
   and dominance of markets 165
   and growth 150, 152, 153, 155
   Marx's ideas on 150
   Schumpeter's ideas on 152
   in Solow's model 153, 155
   see also new technology
technology shocks 111, 112–13, 120, 198
television sets 102, 167
Thailand, growth forecasts 79–80
Thames Valley University 64–5
Thatcher, Margaret xii, 28, 33
The Theory of the Leisure Class (Veblen) 59
Thurow, Lester 25
time domain 118
Tobin, James 148
toy industry ix–x, xi, 61
trade 149, 176n
   intervention 25, 26–7
   in nineteenth-century USA 25–6, 162
   reduction of barriers 98, 135, 136
   restrictions 25–6
   see also free trade
training see education and training
Trainspotting (film) 38
transport, infrastructure 21
travel, in early nineteenth century 145
Twain, Mark 111, 119

uncertainty, and economics ix, 67–8, 102,
      107, 121, 124, 127–8, 129, 135, 136,
      137–8, 188, 200
unemployment 91, 92, 93, 188–9
   and crime 40
   effect of supply and demand 101
   government policy 189
   high levels 94, 188–9
   and inflation 100, 102, 187, 189
   in recessions 188, 189
   reductions 100, 102
uni-variate models 90n, 196
United Artists 13
United Kingdom

change in growth and profitability 98,
      99–100, 136–7, *136*
   divorce rates 50
   elections 29–32
   family structure 53–8
   GDP *81*, 87, 88–9, *88*
   high interest rates 185
   long-term growth 143, 175
   macro-economic forecasts 80
   rise in unemployment in mid-1970s 188
   voting behaviour 30–2
   see also Britain
United States of America
   business cycles 112–13, *113*, 118, 122–3,
      122, 130, 131, 134–5, 137, 198, 200
   car industry 167
   change in growth and profitability 98,
      99–100
   crime 33, 43, 45
   criminal justice system 35–6
   currency fluctuations 14, 17
   divorce rates 50
   empirical testing 157–8
   employment rates 100
   estimated size of economy 146, 148
   family structures 47
   Federal Reserve 89, 186–7
   film industry 12–13
   GDP 193, *194*
   GNP 88–9, *89*, 113–14, *113*, 116–19,
      193–5, *193*, *194*, 197
   government spending xii
   growth rate 98, *99*, 103–4, *104*, 122–3,
      122, 131, *134*, 176
   largest companies 168–9, 178–9, 190
   long-term growth 142–3, *142*, 158, 175,
      177
   low inflation 100, 101, 187
   macro-economic forecasts 80
   Marshall Plan 98, 186
   military technology 159
   New Deal xii
   nineteenth-century trade policies 25–6,
      162
   output 160, 161, 164
   pest control strategies 20–1
   predictability of economy 88–9, 90, 133
   Presidential elections 29, 35
   price stability 186–7
   prisons policy 33, 35–6
   RBC theory and empirical evidence 112,
      137